THE PRINCIPLES

OF THE

ART OF CONVERSATION

Owing to the antiquity and rarity of this book, certain pages are regrettably absent, and readability is compromised due to the blurring of the original text. If you possess any insights regarding the availability of these missing sections, kindly inform us. Your assistance is crucial in ensuring the completion of this significant work for the benefit of future generations.

THE PRINCIPLES

OF THE

ART OF CONVERSATION

BY

J. P. MAHAFFY

GYAN

Published by

Gyan Publishing House
5, Ansari Road
Daryaganj, New Delhi-110002
Phone: 011-47034999, 9811692060
E-mail: books@gyanbooks.com

Distribution Network
gyanbooks.com
India, USA, Canada, UK, Australia

ISBN: 978-93-6208-215-2 (HB)
First Published, 1887

2nd Impression 2024

Printed at: Gyan Press, Delhi.

THE PRINCIPLES OF THE ART OF CONVERSATION
Author: J. P. MAHAFFY

THE PRINCIPLES

OF THE

ART OF CONVERSATION

THE PRINCIPLES

OF THE

ART OF CONVERSATION

BY

J. P. MAHAFFY

London

MACMILLAN AND CO.

AND NEW YORK

1887

PREFACE

PREFACE

If the reader should inquire what special claims the present author can put forward to treat so complex and indeed novel a subject, the first reply is, of course, that he has thought a long time and with much care about it, and this, for a theorist, is sufficient vindication. But it may fairly be added that a writer on the principles of conversation ought to live in a country where the practice of it is confessedly on a high level, and where the average man is able to talk well. This is an additional justification. Lastly, though examples cannot teach the art, it is to be expected that the writer should not live altogether in his study, but should go out and hear as many good conversations as possible, in order to bring his theories to the practical test. These three conditions having been honestly fulfilled, the failure of the book will rather be due to want of ability than to want of honest preparation in the author.

The generality of the treatment may perhaps mislead the reader to think that there is nothing but speculation attempted. This is not so, each single case of general description being drawn from instances under the author's own observation, so that not a few will be recognised by those who have moved in the same society. But, if justly drawn, they ought to be found in every society.

In seeking for advice among those whose conversation has supplied the best materials for his theory, the author has been fortunate enough to obtain the assistance of the MARCHIONESS OF LONDONDERRY and LADY AUDREY BULLER, who have made suggestions and criticisms which he here cordially acknowledges.

TRINITY COLLEGE, DUBLIN,
September 1887.

ANALYSIS

Introduction.

Conversation (1) is universal;
(2) is necessary; and therefore
(3) Is it an art? (§ 2)
(4) Can it be improved?

The great difficulty is this: that it must seem to be natural, and not an art. Hence—

(5) Analogy of the arts of logic and rhetoric (§§ 3, 4), viz.—

(α) They can never be taught without natural gifts to receive them.
(β) They can always be greatly improved in those who possess these gifts.
(γ) They must not be paraded, or they cease to be arts in the higher sense, for
(δ) The highest art is to attain perfect nature.

So also—

(1) No teaching by mere specimens and by memory is possible (§ 5).
(2) All the general rules are obvious, and yet
(3) Natural gifts are necessary to apply them with skill.

I. The Manner of Conversation, or

Subjective Conditions,

(A) in the speaker, and these are either—

(α) Physical, viz. (1) A sweet tone of voice (§ 6).
(2) Absence of local accent.
(3) Absence of tricks and catch-words (§ 7).

or

(β) Mental, viz. (1) Knowledge, which may be either General (books, men), or Special (great topics, the topic of the day).
(2) Quickness.

or

(γ) Moral, viz. (1) Modesty.
(2) Simplicity—digression on Shyness and Reserve.
(3) Unselfishness.
(4) Sympathy.
(5) Tact.

Digression as regards Conditions—
(α) too general—Moral Worth and Truthfulness.
(β) too special—Wit and Humour.

Objective Conditions,

(B) in the hearers, which are either in—
(1) Quantity, for we speak with (α) one, (β) a few, (γ) many.
(2) Quality, for we speak with (α) equals, (β) superiors, (γ) inferiors.
(3) Differences (A) of age, (1) older, (2) younger, (3) equal; (B), of sex—men and women.
(4) Degrees of Intimacy, (α) relations, (β) friends, (γ) acquaintances (familiar, slight).

II. The Matter of Conversation, or

(C) The Topics, which are either—
In Quantity—infinite.
In Quality—serious or trivial.
In Relation—personal or general.

(D) The handling of the Topics must be either—
Deliberative, or by all the company.
Controversial, or by two speakers.
Epideictic, or by one.

Epilogue.

THE PRINCIPLES

OF THE

ART OF CONVERSATION

INTRODUCTION

§ 1. THERE can be no doubt that of all the accomplishments prized in modern society that of being agreeable in conversation is the very first. It may be called the social result of Western civilisation, beginning with the Greeks. Whatever contempt the North American Indian or the Mohammedan Tartar may feel for talking as mere chatter, it is agreed among us that people must meet frequently, both men and women, and that not only is it agreeable to talk, but that it is a matter of common courtesy to say something, even when there is hardly anything to say. Every civilised man and woman feels, or ought to feel, this duty; it is the universal accomplishment which all must practise, and as those who fail signally to attain it are punished by the dislike or neglect of society, so those who succeed beyond the average receive a just reward, not only in the constant pleasure they reap from it, but in the esteem which they gain from their fellows. Many men and many women owe the whole of a great success in life to this and nothing else. An agreeable young woman will always carry away the palm in the long run from the most brilliant player or singer who has nothing to say. And though men are supposed to succeed in life by dead knowledge, or by acquaintance with business, it is often by their social qualities, by their agreeable way of putting things, and not by their more ponderous merits that they prevail.

In the high profession of diplomacy, both home and foreign, this is pre-eminently the case.

But quite apart from all these serious profits, and better than them all, is the daily pleasure derived from good conversation by those who can attain to it themselves or enjoy it in others. It is a perpetual intellectual feast, it is an ever-ready recreation, a deep and lasting comfort, costing no outlay but that of time, requiring no appointments but a small company, limited neither to any age nor any sex, the delight of prosperity, the solace of adversity, the eternal and essential expression of that social instinct which is one of the strongest and best features in human nature.

§ 2. If such be the universality and the necessity of conversation in modern society, it seems an obvious inquiry whether it can be taught or acquired by any fixed method; or rather, as everybody has to practise it in some way, not as a mere ornament, but as a necessity of life, it may be asked: Is there any method by which we can improve our conversation? Is there any theory of it which we can apply in our own case and that of others? If not, are there at least some practical rules which we ought to know, and which we should follow in endeavouring to perform this essential part of our social duties?

To assert that there is some such systematic analysis of conversation possible is to assert that it is an *Art*—a practical science like the art of reasoning called Logic, or the art of eloquence called Rhetoric. Now this runs counter to one of the strongest convictions of all intelligent men and women, that if anything in the world ought to be spontaneous it is conversation. How can a thing be defined by rules which consists in following the chances of the moment, drifting with the temper of the company, suiting the discourse to whatever subject may turn up? The instant any one is felt to be talking by rules all the charm of his society vanishes, and he becomes the worst of social culprits—a bore. For it is the natural easy flow of talk which is indeed the perfection of what we seek. Didactic teaching, humorous anecdotes, clever argument—these may take their part in social intercourse, but they are not its perfection. To take up what others say in easy comment, to give in return something which will please, to stimulate the silent and the morose out of their vapours and surprise them into good-humour, to lead while one seems to follow—this is the real aim of good conversation. How can such a Protean impalpable acquirement be in any way an art depending on rules? Does it not altogether depend on natural gifts, on a ready power of expression, on a sanguine temperament, on a quick power of sym-

gers.[1] It marks a man as provincial, and hence is akin to vulgarity and narrowness of mind. It suggests too that the speaker has not moved much about the world, or even in the best society of his native country, in which such provincialism is carefully avoided, and set down as an index of mind and manners below the highest level. Hence all careful educators endeavour to eradicate peculiarities of accent or pronunciation in children, and justly, though we have all met great talkers whose Scotch burr or Irish brogue seemed an essential feature of their charm. If this be so, no education can eradicate it. In lesser people to be provincial is distinctly an obstacle in the way, even though

[1] It has been suggested to me that a slight impediment or stammer often gives peculiar zest to conversation. But this is hardly the case at first hearing; it is only appreciated when we have discovered that what the speaker is hesitating to utter is worth waiting for. It then produces the same kind of surprise that irony does, which is often deliberate mental stammering.

a great mind may turn it into a stepping-stone.

§ 7. There is yet another almost physical disability or damage to conversation, which is akin to provincialism, and which consists in disagreeable tricks in conversation, such as the constant and meaningless repetition of catchwords and phrases, such as the unmeaning oaths of our grandfathers, such as inarticulate sounds of assent, such as contortions of the face, which so annoy the hearer by their very want of meaning and triviality as to excite quite a disproportionate dislike to the speaker, and to, require great and sterling qualities to counterbalance it. However apt a man's internal furniture may be for conversation, he may make it useless by being externally disagreeable, and how often when we praise a friend as a good talker do we hear the reply: I should like him well enough if he did not worry me with his *don't you know*, or his *what*, or his *exactly so*, or something else so childishly small, that we shudder to think how easily a man may forfeit his position or popularity among civilised men in their daily intercourse. But modern society, which ought to be of all things in human life the most easy and unconstrained, is growing every day more tyrannical and only to be kept in good humour by careful attention to its unwritten behests, unless indeed we have the power to bend it to our will, and force it to follow our lead instead of driving us along like slaves.

No more need be said concerning these physical conditions, which are rather negative conditions, or favourable starting points, than real aids for our purpose. The handsomest man or woman, even with the sweetest tones of human voice, will soon be found out, if dull or unsympathetic, and then these advantages all go for nothing.

MENTAL CONDITIONS—SPECIAL KNOWLEDGE

§ 8. Far more important than the physical gifts of nature, which can only be slightly improved, though they can be completely marred by habit, are the mental conditions of conversation. Among these the most obvious is, of course, Knowledge. An ignorant man is seldom agreeable in conversation, except as a butt; a man full of knowledge is certain to be agreeable if he will conform to the other conditions of the game. The word *knowledge* is, however, so vague, that we must be at pains to define more particularly its divisions, and consider what kind of knowledge is most conducive to good conversation.

Of course the first question suggested to the reader is whether general or special knowledge in the speaker is to be preferred.

There are arguments in favour of each. Let us take the specialist first. There is undoubtedly a great satisfaction in talking to a man who is master of any special subject, even if it be remote from ordinary life. Intelligent questions will draw from the astronomer, from the chemist, possibly from the pure mathematician, curious facts and interesting views on the progress of discovery, which will pleasantly beguile the time even in a light-minded and frivolous company. This opens a field for conversation which is inaccessible if there be no one present to explain or to speak with authority, and so no invitation is more frequent or more welcome than to come and meet a man celebrated in his own line and of wide reputation. The very fact of meeting such a man disposes the company to be sympathetic, and to draw from him the secrets of his knowledge.

This kind of vantage-ground may be

occupied by a man of no original capacity or deep learning, if accident has made him intimate with some exciting or absorbing subject of the day. The man who has just escaped a shipwreck, or fought in a famous battle, or survived some catastrophe, has for the moment the advantage of being endowed with special knowledge, which everybody wants to talk about, and to learn particulars from the actual eyewitness. Akin to this is the advantage of having seen and conversed with the greatest men of the day—a feature which lends the principal charm to those volumes of autobiography or of *recollections*, which approach nearer than any other kind of book to the conditions of a conversation.

§ 9. Of course the danger with either of these specialists, the specialist of a day or the specialist of years, is that he will not leave his subject when it has been sufficiently discussed, as he will probably gauge the interest of others by his own preoccupation, and so may become not a blessing but a bore to his company. Though this is frequently the case, those who have gathered company about them for conversation, and have long experience of what is most likely to succeed, will agree with me that to have a specialist present is always valuable. If other topics flag an appeal to this abundant source will always introduce a new current of talk, and often of the most agreeable kind.

Neither of these mental conditions, which are distinctly valuable in society, include the case of specialists on topics which are of no universal or no permanent interest. Thus there are in English society men devoted to one particular sport or one narrow pursuit, upon which they can talk with authority indeed, and with interest, but only to those who have received the same training. A party of fox-hunters, or racing-men, or college dons, or stockbrokers, who rehearse again in the evening what they have been doing all day, may indeed amuse themselves with talk, but in no sense is it good conversation. One specialist, as I have said, may be of the greatest use in conversation. A set of specialists when they get together are either unintelligible to the average mind or exceedingly tedious.

The same remarks apply to specialists, men or women, who can only discuss topics interesting to one sex. I will not go so far as to say that no conversation can be really good which does not include speakers of both sexes; the divergence in the education and the life of our boys and of our girls is still too wide to make such a limitation reasonable. But it is surely a bad sign of any society to find men's parties considered more agreeable than those of both sexes, for it is a sign either of licence in men's talk or of narrowness in women's education. There are cases of both within most people's experience. The latter is notably the case in some parts of Ireland, and arises from the want of *political* education in Irish women of any but the highest classes. And so it is in many other countries. But this is verging upon the educational conclusions which we must postpone to another occasion.

General Knowledge

§ 10. We come now to the broader condition of General Knowledge. This, in the minds of many, sums up in itself all the conditions of good conversation, and yet it is so partial a truth as to be practically misleading. A great mistake lies at the root of such an opinion, which assumes that the first object of conversation is not to please but to instruct. I could produce one hundred Irish peasants more agreeable than many a highly-informed

Englishman, and yet these peasants might in many cases be unable to read or write. Of course to instruct or to be instructed is often very pleasant, and so far knowledge, general or special, is a very useful help to conversation, but it is as talk, not as a lesson, that we must here regard it.

The advantage of general above special knowledge for our purpose is that it can be applied in a greater number of cases, and used to interest a greater number of people. The man of general knowledge can suit himself to various company, and, if he is not able to speak with the authority of the specialist, can help and stimulate in many cases where the latter is likely to be silent. If therefore we exclude the object of gaining information, which many people estimate above its importance in our present subject, we must decide that general information is the better condition to promote agreeable social intercourse.

It may be attained in two directions; either knowledge of books or knowledge of men. The former is within the reach of most men, even though it requires a peculiar memory to make it applicable with ease and readiness. We may even say with truth that no man can attain to general knowledge nowadays without reading many books. The danger of a desultory habit, very likely to arise from skimming the mass of ephemeral literature now gushing from the press, is that the facts acquired will not be ordered, and will come out as untidy scraps, not as the details of a proper system of study. The books which a man reads may either be the great masters, which are perhaps rather useful for cultivating his deeper self than for ordinary converse, or the newest authors, whose merits are still upon trial, and who therefore afford an excellent field for discussion and criticism. In either case there is hardly a distinction to be drawn between the specialist and the generalist, for all people are supposed to study literature, and a good knowledge of either familiar or fashionable books can hardly fail to tell in any gathering of cultivated men and women.

§ 11. There is, however, another kind of general knowledge which is not so easy to acquire, for it requires long experience, a certain position in society, and means for foreign travel. I mean the general knowledge of remarkable men, concerning whom the speaker can tell his recollections. There is often a man of no great learning or ability whose official position, tact, or private means have brought him into contact with the great minds about whom every detail is interesting. Such a man's general knowledge should always make him an agreeable member of society. Akin to this man is the experienced traveller who has wandered through many lands and seen the cities and the ways of men.

The peculiar advantage of this kind of general knowledge for conversation is that its very acquisition comes in the practice of society, and that all those defects of narrowness, awkwardness, and self-consciousness which often mar the man of books, are rubbed off, as the phrase is, by constant contact with various men. The man of books, on the contrary, has to acquire his store in the silence of his study, and so by a process which rather untrains him for talking, so that even though his knowledge when acquired may be of more solid and permanent value, his way of producing it may put him at a disadvantage.

Let me add before leaving this head that the enormous increase of the means for acquiring knowledge, and the application of great inventions to save time in so doing, are by no means accompanied by corresponding strides in the art of conversation. All the knowledge of the day professes to be curtailed and collected into newspapers, periodicals, and handbooks, just as all the travelling of the day is done by rail and steam, with the aid of guide-books, which save the traveller all the trouble and all the education of thinking. The tourist who formerly went through Italy with his *vetturino*, and saw every village and road deliberately, talking with the people and observing national life, is now whirled through tunnels and by night from one capital to another, where he sees what Cook or Murray choose him to see, just as the man who trusts the newspapers for his knowledge gets scraps, perversions, even lies, served up for him by way of universal information. It is easy to see that this kind of training, as it interferes with both liberty and leisure of thought, and induces men to spend far too much time in gathering facts, is in no way conducive to the improvement of conversation.

INTELLECTUAL QUICKNESS

§ 12. What has hitherto been said about knowledge in a man of conversation has left out of all account the way of producing it, and merely considered the mental store from which conversation may be supplied. But almost as important as these materials, is the faculty of producing them without effort. This quality may be called intellectual *quickness*, as distinguished from solidity; and of all the conditions we have yet discussed, this seems most due to nature, and unattainable by education. It is indeed sometimes a characteristic of nations. The Irishman or the Frenchman will show this quality with an average excellence far above that attained in England or Germany. It may of course be allied with, or even due to, some such moral quality as sympathy, of which we shall speak presently. But quite apart from it, a selfish man, who has no sympathy for his company, may, by the quickness of his intellect, show brilliantly in conversation, while his more solid and worthy fellow is considered a bore. As I have just said, this is generally a gift of nature. Some men and some nations are born with quick wits. But even so it is a great mistake to think that it may not be vastly improved by intercourse with people who have the faculty already well developed. Moreover it is a very dangerous advantage, and if not deepened by solid acquirements, or chastened by moral restraints, may make a man rather the scourge than the delight of his company.

For this is the mental quality which is the foundation of wit, and a joker who merely consults his own amusement, or the amusement of some of his hearers at the expense of others, is not a good converser. The tendency of a very quick intellect is also to impatience, and so it will interfere with and cow more modest minds, which might have contributed well to the feast of talk had they been allowed to work without hurry or pressure. So strong do we often find this contrast that it is unadvisable, in choosing a set of people for conversation, to bring together very slow and very quick intellects. While the former are more dazzled and confused than pleased, the latter feel the delay of listening to long and deliberate sentences intolerable; and so a company in which all the members are socially excellent may fail to be pleasant on account of the mental contrasts of its members.

Let me illustrate it by an extreme case. Who would think of introducing a young brilliant flashing sceptic into a society of grave and sober orthodoxy? If the conversation did not soon degenerate into acrid controversy—the very lees of social intercourse—it would result in contemptuous silence on one side or other, probably with the contempt so transparent as to challenge harsh over-statement from the talker by way of challenge or reply to unspoken censure. Could anything be more ruinous to the object we have in view? It may be urged on the other hand that if too many quick intellects are brought together—not a very easy thing, by the way, to accomplish—the pressure will become too great and the conversation move so fast that the strain may become a weariness. I think that any danger in this direction is rather due to the moral defects of the talkers than their intellectual brightness, and so I shall discuss this point under another head.

But if the quality under consideration is valuable at all times, it is so peculiarly when a number of strangers meet together, or when it is the lot of men and women to be obliged to talk together in dialogue, upon a stray or sudden occasion. Then it is, when for example you go down to dinner with a strange man or woman whose name you have not caught, that quickness of intellect becomes the prime agent in starting a pleasant conversation. There are, indeed, even here many easy rules which may help to get over the initial difficulty, without those initial chords about the weather whereby so many people, otherwise really intelligent, hide themselves at the outset under the prelude of commonplace. But here as elsewhere art can only imitate better nature.

It is further to be added that as general knowledge, and special also, are principally to be expected from men, so quickness of mind, which is often impaired by deeper study, is the proper attribute of women, and ought to be the distinctive quality of their conversation. This is supposed to be so in French society; I cannot say that it has come under my observation as a general law, the many instances which I have met being always noted and quoted as brilliant and as exceptional, so implying that it was not the rule.

MORAL CONDITIONS—MODESTY

§ 13. We may now pass from the intellectual conditions of conversation to what I may call, for simplicity's sake, the moral conditions. It is, of course, certain that these so-called moral qualities are frequently congenital or constitutional, and that, therefore, the owner of them deserves no credit for possessing them. But as they are qualities enjoined upon us by moralists, and are in any case analogous to moral virtues, we may in this book, which does not affect precise philosophy, class them as moral. For example, the instinct of sociality, which is really the same as the gregarious instinct in birds and animals, is not the same as the love of our neighbour enjoined by the Gospel, but is closely connected with it, for to be social without being civil is not possible, and civility is at least the imitation of friendship, if it be not friendship or benevolence in outward acts of social intercourse. This, too, appears to be the reason why a particular class of social instincts is so agreeable to men, and so honoured in society—their close relationship to moral virtues.

Let me take up the first and most obvious—Modesty.[1] It is quite certain that modesty and its opposite are congenital to various people. Those who have to do with the education of children can see it within the limits of a family, not to say a school. Some boys and girls are naturally retiring, and think little of their

[1] I include here under the word all its various gradations from mere bashfulness to that moral self-restraint which makes us fear to assert ourselves, as implying an over-estimate of our powers.

powers; others are the reverse. But here too, as we all know, early education may make great changes. A child not originally remarkable in either way may be unduly brought forward and applauded, or again unduly repressed and cowed, so that the constant habit of early years may actually modify the original character in either of two opposite directions. But this is only possible when the original nature is not strongly declared; if it be so, I hold education to be almost helpless.

When the child is growing to maturity it is likely to be strongly affected by watching the defects of others, or hearing the frequent censure of them. Thus I see that the children of people with too much manner are apt to have no manner at all (as the phrase is), and the children of incessant talkers are so bored with this social vice that they never think of practising talk during the absence of their parents. Let us apply these remarks to modesty.

§ 14. There is no quality in man, still more in woman, which is more attractive and which commands more respect. Every intelligent and sympathetic person makes allowance for it, and strives to lessen the necessary pains which it inflicts upon the possessor of it in society. It is akin to simplicity and honesty, and opposed to that artificiality which is the outward and visible sign of some kind of dishonesty. It lends a charm to youth and inexperience, so that people who are wearied with the labours of talking to worn and world-stained equals feel, as it were, the breath of gorse and heather after the odours of city air when they come in contact with genuine modesty. It is a quality sometimes allied with that heaven-born genius which attains great results without apparent effort, and, therefore, is not infected with the pride of having gained conscious and hard-fought successes. It is, lastly, the outcome of great and solid labour, which teaches the specialist how much he fails to know, and the general student how small a fragment of human knowledge he has compassed. Here it is no natural quality, but an acquired virtue; yet it excites the same kind of feeling in society.

There is, therefore, no quality more highly valuable in society and more certain, *within limits*, to conduce to agreeable conversation. Perhaps the clearest reservation, and one which will cover almost all the various cases, is this: *modesty without simplicity*, though it may still be a moral virtue, is always a social vice; and therefore highly detrimental to good conversation; for as soon as modesty becomes conscious, it assumes one of two forms—the parade of apology or the cloak of reserve.

I need hardly insist that the man or

woman who displays modesty by constantly apologising for native ignorance or stupidity injures conversation, and can only amuse a company by becoming ridiculous. What we want to learn from each member is his free opinion on the subject in hand, not his own estimate of the value of that opinion. How evidently this is a social vice will appear from the fact that an assumption of this kind of modesty is one of the commonest and most diverting forms of humour—I mean the irony which has been the helper of conversation ever since the days of Socrates, as we find him in Plato's *Dialogues.*

MORAL CONDITIONS—SIMPLICITY

§ 15. We cannot analyse the second form of conscious modesty, Reserve, till we have said a few words on the virtue akin to modesty which reserve particularly violates, I mean of the quality of Simplicity. It is a great mistake to say that simplicity as such is always a virtue. There is for example the *enfant terrible* who upsets everybody and causes shocking shame and confusion by the indiscreet directness of his inquiries. The very same kind of mistake is made by grown people who are ignorant of the ways of society, such as country girls, or girls of an inferior rank,. who are married into a cultivated society, and who are allowed such liberties, either for their beauty's sake, or for novelty's sake, that they announce whatever comes into their head, and disturb conversation by their irrelevancy and shallowness, if not by suggesting subjects undesirable in general society. There is also the blunt man, whose simplicity takes the form of rudeness, who thinks it more important that he should speak out the plain truth, than that he should spare the feelings of others. This is again a vice parading under the form of a virtue—perhaps here of truthfulness rather than simplicity, but the two are so akin that at this point we need not draw distinctions. The conversational side of truthfulness is after all little more than directness and simplicity of utterance.

So far then I have put the defects of simplicity first, because they are more likely to be overlooked than its advantages. When, therefore, these important limitations are made, and they affect a great number of cases, we must admit that there is the greatest charm in simplicity, in the temper which without assumption of ignorance, or parade of inexperience, opens a candid eye of inquiry upon the company, receives with readiness new information, and is ready to tell without conceits or ornaments the actual impressions in the speaker's mind.

It may be found not only along with genius, which is often of this character, but along with great experience and acuteness; we hear for example, that it is the leading characteristic of Prince Bismarck's conversation. I remember it likewise with delight in the conversation of the late Isaac Butt, an Irish genius of the highest order, and a talker second to none, whose life was stormy, and whose character not by any means such as would naturally imply this quality of simplicity. On the other hand, it is quite extravagant to postulate it as a necessary sign of genius, and to say that those who are wanting in it are certainly wanting either in ability or honesty. There are great minds naturally wanting in simplicity, just as there are great minds wanting in modesty or in truthfulness—such as J. J. Rousseau and the great Napoleon in the latter two, and one great English writer of our day in the former, whom I need not name. Human nature will not be tied down in any such fetters.

But when all has been said that can be said on either side, it will remain certain that the man who appears simple, and who therefore affects his company with the impression that they are in direct contact with his mind, has a distinct advantage over those who either from conceits of style, or over-delicacy of sentiment, or education in an artificial atmosphere, appear with their minds, as it were, dressed or tattooed, and not in the purity of nature.

I need hardly add that it is necessary to sever simplicity from modesty as social qualities, since the one may even contradict the other, though they are so often in harmony. The blunt man above mentioned, who speaks out his mind with over-simplicity, may be very devoid of modesty, and conversely there are certain phases of modesty, such as *prudery*, which make the speaker avoid simplicity, and cover his meaning by various subterfuges. It is when the two qualities work together, and appear habitual to the speaker, that they produce their admirable effect. If he is narrating, for example, a tragic history, or story of adventure in which he has taken part, while his modesty will prevent him from magnifying his own share in the matter, and so trying to the utmost the faith of his hearers, his simplicity will prevent him from unduly concealing his action, and will ensure that he tells the whole truth, so far as he knows it. If again he be asked his opinion on a question which he has studied, and upon which he ought to be an authority, his modesty may prevent him from giving the company the benefit of his knowledge, unless his simplicity makes him attend directly to the matter in hand, and not to the position of referee in which he suddenly comes to be placed.

Moral Conditions—Shyness Reserve

§ 16. We have kept till now the main violation of simplicity, and greatest of modern hindrances to conversation, which we have already mentioned in connection with modesty.

What distinction are we to make between Shyness and reserve, two qualities whose effects are generally similar, and each of which is a great hindrance to good conversation? We may start from the distinctions in ordinary use. No man or woman will openly claim to be reserved, but many will plead that they are shy. The reason of this is that shyness is assumed to be a physical or at least constitutional thing, whereas reserve implies deliberate choice to stand aloof, and repel any intimacy of conversation as unwarranted either by the circumstances or by the relative position of the speakers. Thus though reserve *may* arise from modesty, it is generally a form of pride, which for that reason no one will attribute to himself.[1] On the other hand shyness is either assumed to be a form, or an excess, of modesty, which is a virtue, or it is assumed to be congenital, and therefore a defect to be excused rather than a fault to be censured. So shy people as a rule rather 'fancy themselves'; for though they urge their peculiarity as an excuse for social defects, there lies behind a secret conviction that they at least have escaped the vice of forwardness, or of that coarseness of mental fibre which is implied in forwardness. Accordingly, though there

[1] I am reminded that there are, especially in England, people who desire to be thought reserved, and are secretly proud of this reputation. It is, of course, part of this pride not to declare it publicly. These exceptional cases are, however, to be classed with those of people who are secretly proud of other vices, and do not disturb my theory.

are many people who sincerely regret their shyness upon particular occasions, as for example, when they are compelled to make a speech, or entertain some great personage, yet you will not find any one who would exchange it as a permanent quality for perfect ease, or assurance, or total absence of nervousness, or whatever else the opposite of shyness may be called. The more we reflect on this and other similar symptoms in shyness, the more we shall be convinced that here we have not to deal with mere modesty, but with conscious modesty, with modesty without simplicity, and therefore really with a subtle form of conceit.

§ 17. There are of course cases of children who are allowed to run away whenever a stranger appears, as if nature were a state of war, and man the natural enemy of man. Such children will require training to be cured of their own and their parents' stupidity, and must be taught that every stranger is not a bogy. But this is mere domestication, such as we apply to the lower animals. It is also possible, though rare, that some people of refinement and culture may have a physical repugnance to meeting any but their intimates, and that they may make honest efforts in vain to overcome this stubborn nervousness. The great majority of shy people are not of this kind. Thus you will see a girl extremely shy in ordinary society, who blossoms out when she receives attentions from some one who may possibly marry her. Or else you may find a youth, who jumps over a hedge to avoid meeting a party of his acquaintances on a country road, anything but modest in lower society, thus showing that it is a consciousness of unfitness for good company and a fear of being criticised which dominate him. In almost all the cases which occur there is therefore modesty without simplicity, a conscious and almost guilty air; it is often nothing better than vanity which fears the results of conversation, which desires to be thought well of, and which from mistrust of itself puts on the garb of modesty.

If shyness really arises from this cause, it is a grave moral fault. But in any case it is socially a crime. How can any conversation be easy and natural, how can it range from topic to topic, and bring out the tempers and the characters of the speakers, if any of them displays this vice by dogged silence, by conscious blushing when any personal topic arises, or by the awkwardness which always accompanies this noisome preoccupation with one's self? If then the capital conditions of pleasant intercourse are modesty and simplicity, this defect which always contradicts the latter, and generally both of them, is to be regarded as the most prevalent and destructive anti-social vice. The only high quality which may be concealed, or perhaps even displayed by shyness, is a delicate sensitiveness, which shy people generally postulate in themselves, but which has far better and nobler ways of affecting society than by impeding conversation.

§ 18. Reserve, which few venture to claim for themselves, is a far higher and better feeling, for it implies that the unwillingness to enter upon conversation arises from some deliberate judgment as to the relative positions of the speaker and his company—often a correct judgment, saving us from the vice of familiarity, which in an inferior is offensive, in a superior uncomfortable, in either case distinctly vulgar. We feel that reserve can be laid aside in pleasant moments, and among congenial people, and that there is often force and dignity behind it. But it is rarely a virtue which improves conversation, and therefore need not occupy us here. It may indeed act as a check on licence, and so by bringing the company back from some aberration, start it afresh on nobler and pleasanter topics. This is so indirect a mode of action, and may be so much more easily attained in other ways, that I need only mention it for completeness' sake.

Unselfishness

§ 19. Next to modesty and simplicity I class the moral virtue of *unselfishness.* It is very characteristic that we have no other word for this noble quality than the mere negation of its opposite—the most prevalent vice in the world. Why can we not describe it better? Because in particular connections it has other names—loyalty, devotion, self-sacrifice, which occupy a part of the ground with more especial attributes. We are not here concerned with these heights of human nature, with the nobility of grand and pathetic moments. What shows itself in these as devotion and self-sacrifice bears in our commonplace life a negative and non-descriptive name, and is yet a very distinct and valuable quality, distinct from simplicity, distinct even from sympathy, with which it is so often allied; it may display itself in all kinds of men and women who take part in a conversation. It is not less important to the silent man than to the talkative man, though the latter case is the more obvious. The good talker who monopolises conversation, who insists on keeping other people waiting that he may finish his story, who tells anecdotes which are evidently unpleasant to some of the company, but will not forego his joke for the sake of others—the social bully who makes butts of the more retiring, and sallies at their expense, is the most obvious case of a man failing from selfishness, and losing the great natural advantages he possesses through want of the opposite quality. This is the man too who interrupts others, who refuses to exercise for a moment that patience which he so often exacts.

I have spoken of these people as failures, and such they really are, in the truest and highest sense, for they certainly kill more conversation than they create, nor do they understand that the very meaning of the word implies a contribution-feast, an *eranos* as the Greeks would say, not the entertainment provided by a single host. But alas! in a lesser and looser sense these people often dominate society for years, and are even sought out as social conveniences, who will keep things going at a dinner table, and supply the defects of silence and dulness so painfully common in English more than in other societies. But the punishment of the selfish talker is sure to come at last, when he lives till his vivacity and his power of acquiring new things fail, while he still presumes on his old reputation. He is then discovered to be an intolerable bore, which, indeed from a higher point of view, was always the case; and thereupon society, which is as selfish as he is, and insists on being amused at all costs, throws him aside with contempt. He has perhaps still one place of refuge; he may become a high priest in that great modern temple of selfishness—his club; but even there his popularity has waned, and he sinks into the old age unfriended and unsociable —*ἄφιλον ἀπροσόμιλον*—which Sophocles regarded as one of the tragic features in the life of man.

§ 20. I turn now to a far more common, but less observed and less censured case of social selfishness, which requires urgently to be brought into the light of criticism. No man requires to practise unselfishness more than the silent man; for as everybody is able to contribute and ought to contribute something, so the man who thrusts himself into society to enjoy the talk of others, and will take no trouble to help, to suggest, or to encourage, is really a serious criminal. I have known a person of good position, and not the least wanting in brains, who would insist in sitting at dinner between the two most agreeable people in the room, in order that he might eat and listen, while under no circumstances would he make the smallest effort to entertain in return. These silent people not only take all they can get in society for nothing, but they take it without the smallest gratitude, and have the audacity afterwards to censure those who have laboured for their amusement.

I ask the reader's pardon for illustrating this important fact by a personal anecdote. In a country house where I was staying, the host had invited the colonel commanding a neighbouring depôt and his wife to dinner, and the conversation was flagging seriously. Some mention of New Zealand in that day's papers suggested it as a topic, upon which a couple of us brought out all we knew about New Zealand, discussed the natives, then savages generally, and so restored the fortunes of the evening. The colonel and his wife still sat silent. When they were gone, we said to the host that we thought it very hard work to entertain people who would not say anything to anybody. He replied that they *had* said something as they got into their carriage. What was it? The colonel observed that it was very impertinent of people to talk about countries they had never seen, especially in presence of a man like himself, who had not only lived for years in New Zealand, but had written a book about it! This was the thanks we got.

§ 21. There is another special scope for unselfishness in society, which may fitly find its place here. In every company there may be people either socially or intellectually inferior to the rest, who feel themselves somewhat *out of it* (to use a vulgar phrase), and whom the selfish man, the big talker, the ambitious man is apt to ignore. And yet these very people may be in possession of knowledge or of mental qualities which will be of the highest value in conversation. It requires unselfishness to watch them, to appeal to their sympathies, to draw them into the stream and make them feel that instead of being outsiders they are really among people anxious to know what they think and hear what they have to say. Many a time have I seen an unknown and obscure person drawn in this way and become the leading feature in a delightful evening, for fresh and curious knowledge, which suddenly springs from an unexpected source, can hardly fail to be profoundly interesting, and to stimulate all the active minds that hear it. Thus I remember a stupid young man successfully probed by an intelligent person, till it accidentally came out that he knew all about the wild cattle in Lord Tankerville's park (Chillingham Forest). From that moment he took the lead in the conversation, and excited a most interesting discussion, in which several very dull country farmers took an animated interest.

All this can be done by mere intellectual unselfishness, by the man or woman who considers that each person in a society should be attended to, and if possible compelled to contribute to the general entertainment. But it is both rare to find this kind of unselfishness and difficult to apply it without the subsidiary faculty or constitution of mind, which many think the whole root of good conversation—I mean sympathy.

SYMPATHY

§ 22. The great Adam Smith, in a book called *Moral Sentiments*, which he seems to have thought out as a sort of antidote to the selfishness of the *Wealth of Nations*,[1] managed to deduce all the virtues from this one root of sympathy. Starting from the fact that man is a gregarious animal, with social instincts, he showed that the desire to be in sympathy with our fellow-creatures, and so command their love and respect, made us watch them, consider what they felt about us, and avoid everything which might shock or hurt their opinions or their feelings. It was this indefinite and impersonal public opinion which was by degrees made a part of ourselves, and under the

[1] Cf. on the relation of these two books, the highly interesting passage in H. T. Buckle's chapter on the development of the Scotch intellect in his famous *History of Civilisation*.

name of conscience was set up as 'a man within the breast' of each of us to approve and disapprove even our most secret actions.

I quote this once famous theory here, to show how a great thinker, probably the greatest of his age, estimated the force and influence of sympathy; and whatever exaggerations he may have made concerning it in the province of morals, it seems hard to over-estimate it in the province of social intercourse. The first condition of any conversation at all, is that people should have their minds so far in sympathy that they are willing to talk upon the same subject, and to hear what each member of the company thinks about it. The higher condition which now comes before us is, that the speaker, apart from the matter of the conversation, feels an interest in his hearers as distinct persons, whose opinions and feelings he desires to know.

This is the real secret of the power of personal beauty in society. Only a very small number of people will fall in love with each beautiful man or woman. But nearly every one will be so far attracted by beauty that he will pay attention to what the beautiful person says, and feel a keen interest to know what mind and temper accompanies such perfection of form. Thus personal beauty secures the sympathy of any company, so much so, that even when found out to be a mere shell, with no mental force behind it, the attraction lasts, and lends some charm to what would otherwise be called trivial and stupid. This natural sympathy with beauty of external form is a sort of symbol of the feeling which seeks for any mental beauty or advantage to be found in a company, and by showing an interest in it, disposes the possessor of it to expand and become friendly in response to such appreciation. The sympathetic man will feel that his company talk best about the things they know best, or have had special opportunities of learning, and he will be naturally anxious to find the best side of them, and to exhibit it by his suggestions. And as in every conversation there must not only be good talking but good listening, the intellectual gifts which make the talker are often marred if he has not the sympathy which makes the listener.

This remark suggests that the social virtues of the sexes are broadly distinguished by some such principle. Women ought not to be obliged to lead in a conversation, but it will grow dry and dull if they are not ready with their sympathy to hear what is said with pleasure, and to stimulate others by quick and intelligent appreciation. I have known a clever woman maintain a deservedly high character for her conversation who really said very little, but was so sympathetic that she made her guests eloquent, and thus so thoroughly pleased with themselves, that she was lit up by the glow of their satisfaction, and earned very justly the credit for talking well simply because she made others talk. There is probably no social talent higher than this—or rarer.

§ 23. But I suppose no one will be disposed to dispute this, or to underrate the value of sympathy as a quality for conversation. It is much more likely that people may think to simplify the whole matter by arguing that, with the postulate of some brains and some education, all that is required is sympathy, and the more of it the better, so that nothing else remains to be said. We must, therefore, consider carefully how far this is true, and whether there be not some important limitations which complicate the question.

There is one on the very surface. Sympathy must not be excessive in quality, which makes it demonstrative, and therefore likely to repel its object. We have an excellent word which describes the over-sympathetic person, and marks the judgment of society, when we say that he or she is *gushing*. Of course as women are more frequently endowed with this virtue than men, they also err more frequently in the excess, at least in Teutonic races, for among Latin races a gushing man is quite a common phenomenon. This sort of person not only volunteers to show his sympathy before it is required, and often spoils conversation at the outset, but is ever ready to agree with everybody, so making a discussion, which implies differences in opinion, impossible. There results a social impression of a mixed kind, which is even more disagreeable than downright dislike, and therefore socially worse—I mean that of feeling a dislike and contempt for a person who is known to be full of goodness and benevolence. Many people resent being obliged to confuse their judgment in this way, and feel a stronger antipathy to this marred goodness than to proclaimed evil.

In the next place, sympathy must not be excessive in quantity or indiscriminate, otherwise it ceases to have any great social value. The most seductive way of conveying your sympathy to another is to join with him in some strong antipathy, thus showing that all the world cannot claim your friendship, but that you distribute your likes and dislikes with judgment and discrimination. A man who is known to have a special sympathy for some particular age or sex or class in society is far more agreeable to that class than he who embraces all the world in his affections. Nay, if one usually reserved or shy expands for once, or to some few people, in contrast to his usual habit, this sympathy is indeed treasured as a real token of confidence.

These and many similar observations, which will occur to the intelligent reader, will indicate how important are the limitations of sympathy, and how essential it is that this, like every other social virtue, should be carefully husbanded, and not squandered at random without regard to its value. I should add that the foregoing remarks are specially applicable to English (I do not mean English-speaking) society. There is no people more distant and reserved in social intercourse, or that more resents any display of feeling, most of all of sympathy, without a careful introduction and considerable intimacy among the company. Thus those who are accustomed to freer and more outspoken societies, not to say French and Italian life, may make social mistakes in England on the score of sympathy, which are sins only in the heavy atmosphere of Anglo-Saxon manners.

Moral Conditions—Tact

§ 24. The highest and best of all the moral conditions for conversation is what we call *tact*. I say a condition, for it is very doubtful whether it can be called a single and separate quality; more probably it is a combination of intellectual quickness with lively sympathy. But so clearly is it an intellectual quality, that of all others it can be greatly improved, if not actually acquired, by long experience in society. Like all social excellences it is almost given as a present to some people, while others with all possible labour never acquire it. As in billiard-playing, shooting, cricket, and all these other facilities which are partly mental and partly physical, many never can pass a certain point of mediocrity; but still even those who have the talent must practise it, and only become really distinguished after hard work. So it is in art. Music and painting are not to be attained by the crowd. Not even the just criticism of these arts is attainable without certain natural gifts ; but a great deal of practice in good galleries and at good concerts, and years spent among artists, will do much to make even moderately-endowed people sound judges of excellence.

Tact, which is the sure and quick judgment of what is suitable and agreeable in society, is likewise one of those delicate and subtle qualities or a combination of qualities which is not very easily defined, and therefore not teachable by fixed precepts ; but we can easily see that it is based on all the conditions we have already discussed. Some people attain it through sympathy ; others through natural intelligence; others through a calm temper; others again by observing closely the mistakes of their neighbours. As its name implies, it is a sensitive touch in social matters, which feels small changes of temperature, and so guesses at changes of temper; which sees the passing cloud on the expression of one face, or the eagerness of another that desires to bring out something personal for others to enjoy. This quality of tact is of course applicable far beyond mere actual conversation. In nothing is it more useful than in preparing the right conditions for a pleasant society, in choosing the people who will be in mutual sympathy, in thinking over pleasant subjects of talk and suggesting them, in seeing that all disturbing conditions are kept out, and that the members who are to converse should be all without those small inconveniences which damage society so vastly out of proportion to their intrinsic importance.

§ 25. This social skill is generally supposed to be congenital, especially in some women, and no one thinks of laying down rules for it, as its application is so constant, various, and often sudden. Yet it is certain that any one may improve himself by reflection on the matter, and so avoid those shocking mistakes which arise from social stupidity. Thus in the company of a woman who is a man's third wife, most people will instinctively avoid jokes about Blue Beard, or anecdotes of comparison between a man's several wives, of which so many are current in Ireland. But quite apart from instinct, an experienced man who is going to tell a story which may have too much point for some of those present, will look round and consider each member of the party, and if there be a single stranger there whose views are not familiar to him, he will forego the pleasure of telling the story rather than make the social mistake of hurting even one of the guests. On the other hand, this very example shows how a single stranger may spoil a whole conversation by inducing caution in the speakers and imposing upon them such reserve as is inconsistent with a perfectly easy flow of talk.

Another evidence of tact is the perception that a topic has been sufficiently discussed, and that it is on the point of becoming tedious. There is nothing which elderly people should watch more carefully in themselves, for even those once gay and brilliant are almost certain to become prosy with age, and to dwell upon their favourite topics as if this preference were shared by all society. But even the young must be here perpetually upon the watch, and show their tact by refraining from too many questions or too much argument upon any single subject, which becomes a bore to others.[1] Every

[1] Even too careful an attention to grammar, and the careful rounding of periods in easy intercourse, is apt to be tedious, and should be avoided. The instant the company has grasped your idea, you should pass to something else without regard to the form of your sentence.

host and hostess should make it their first duty to watch this human weakness, and should lead away the conversation when it threatens to stay in the same groove. It is better to do this bluntly and confessedly than to refrain from doing it. But the quality of tact, as it quickly perceives the growing mischief, is also quick of resource in devising such interruptions as may seem natural or unavoidable, so as to beguile the company into new paths, and even make the too persistent members lay aside their threadbare discussion without regret.

Conditions too General—Moral Worth and Truthfulness

§ 26. In all the faculties hitherto enumerated, it has been my principle to select and specify those which are capable of improvement by conscious training. I have over and over again admitted that nature — probably meaning by nature *heredity*—has endowed some people with gifts which others must strive to attain by exercise. But I have hitherto excluded such conditions as are either too wide to be called conditions of conversation, or too special ever to be attained without great and peculiar natural gifts.

Of the first kind are general moral worth and truthfulness, which afford the proper ground for respect, and which therefore give weight and importance to anything the speaker says. In cases of moral doubt, in cases of disputed fact, the authority of such a person is a welcome haven of rest for those that distrust other evidence, and like a great authority in a science expounding the principles of that science, so a man or woman of high character may be of much service in conversation. But of course it would be ridiculous to recommend the cultivation of this lofty character for the sake of conversation. It is perhaps more practical to observe that an over-seriousness in morals may be detrimental to the ease and grace, above all to the playfulness, of talk. Let me not be misunderstood in this matter. There is no more valuable and useful check on the degenerating of talk into ribaldry, profanity, or indecency, than the presence of a mind of solid moral worth, which will not tolerate such licence. There are companies, especially of young men, where such things are taken for wit, and which thus show a degradation of the conception of talk that would very soon render conversation intolerable to any intelligent man, not only from its coarseness, but from its dulness. No man, no society, can be called witty, which has not far better credentials than that. Every company of men ought to import two or three grave and reverend people into their circle for the purpose of checking such ruinous excesses, if there be any probability that the conversation may stray into this slough of mire.

§ 27. But on the other hand, there is such a thing in society—Aristotle saw it long ago—as being over-scrupulous in truthfulness. Even a consummate liar, though generally vulgar, and therefore offensive, is a better ingredient in a company than the scrupulously truthful man, who weighs every statement, questions every fact, and corrects every inaccuracy. In the presence of such a social scourge I have heard a witty talker pronounce it the golden rule of conversation to *know nothing accurately*. Far more important is it, in my mind, to *demand* no accuracy. There is no greater or more common blunder in society than to express disbelief or scepticism in a story told *for the amusement of the company*. The object of the speaker is not to instruct, but to divert, and to ask him: Is that really true? or to exclaim: Really that is too much to expect us to believe! shows that the objector is a blockhead unfit for any amusing conversation. The only social criticism on such a story, if it be really beyond the bounds of reasonable belief, is to out-do it with another still more extravagant, and so to bring back the company with laughter, and by excess of exaggeration to a soberer vein. The seriousness of the blunder just noted is not felt till we have learned that there is a vast number of real facts in nature so strange at first hearing, that they excite active scepticism, and that you may lay a wager with any one to pass them off as lies. In fact, any society only familiar with one class of natural facts, can be furnished with facts from another sphere in nature which the majority will disbelieve.[1]

[1] For example, to men of town life, or of mere books, it will seem incredible that a fish should shoot flies with a drop of water, or a diver carry about its egg hugged

The point of importance in the present connection is that, if a man is reporting what he knows to be true, and finds himself disbelieved, he will certainly either feel hurt, or will conceive such contempt for the ignorance and bad manners of his hearers that he will make no further effort to help the conversation.

The outcome, therefore, of what has here been said about high moral worth and extreme truthfulness, is that these virtues, though lending the speaker dignity, must not be allowed to tyrannise. The great and good man must unbend ; he must acquiesce in being amused ; he must even connive at inaccuracies, and smile at what he considers inventions ; he must for the nonce regard recreation as his direct object.

against its breast, or that an otter should take a single bite out of a salmon and leave the rest, or that a woodcock should carry its young in its bill, all of which facts in natural history I have myself heard told to intelligent pedants, and set down by them as impudent inventions.

CONDITIONS TOO SPECIAL—WIT AND HUMOUR

§ 28. There may have been times and nations where conversation was regarded as so serious and important an engine of education, that sound argument, brilliant illustration, and ample information, took the highest place as qualities of talk. Perhaps they do in some cases now, as, for example, everybody who knows him will concede to Mr. Gladstone the palm as a very charming man in society by reason of these qualities. But among hard-working and somewhat fatigued people, who have been pursuing information of various kinds in all their working hours, conversation must be of the nature of relaxation ; it must be amusing first, tructive afterwards, and so it is that nowadays no qualities, however valuable, rank so high in popular estimation for social purposes, as wit and humour.

I will not ascend to a philosophical analysis of these terms, or attempt to answer the obscure and difficult question: What is it that makes us laugh, and why we seem to have in this somewhat trivial point a special feature distinguishing us from all the lower animals? They may have the faculty of reason; they seem entirely devoid of the faculty of ridicule. Nay, even in the scale of civilisation, it is remarkable that the savage and the ignorant laugh less and understand less of this great fund of enjoyment than civilised people. There are also, of course, national differences. The English boor seldom laughs, and then at very coarse fun; the Italian or the Irishman often, and very innocently; the modern Greek, though highly intelligent and keen, very seldom, apparently from want of taste for the ridiculous.

As regards the distinction between wit and humour, all I need here insist upon is that the former consists in quick flashes, in prompt repartee, in quaint comparison; while the latter is sustained; it is a comic way of looking at serious things, a flavouring of narrative, a perception of a ludicrous vein in human life and character. Both these are now esteemed very highly, perhaps beyond their value, in society, but they are so specially natural gifts, and are so impossible to attain by practice, that they cannot be enjoined as conditions to which every talker must conform; they can only be described, and their force or weakness illustrated.

§ 29. There is nothing that requires to *appear* spontaneous more stringently than either of these qualities, and yet we read of great wits, like Sheridan, who carefully prepared their sallies, and even suborned some one to lead up to them. The effect of knowing this is to detract greatly from the enjoyment of the company, and still more from the reputation of the speaker. Most of us would say, that however brilliant in writing comedies, Sheridan must have been distinctly wanting in that gift of spontaneous and ready wit which flashes out at the least provocation, and is mere intellectual playfulness, like the playfulness of a young and happy animal.

So strongly do we feel this in Irish society, where wit is less uncommon than elsewhere, and where it is no less highly prized, that a kind of social religion warns us not to study it beforehand, and any one suspected of coming out with prepared smart things is received by the company with ridicule. Yet for all that, it cannot possibly be denied that as most of the brilliant things which a man uses in any conversation must be at second hand—to invent such things one after another at the moment being beyond the power of human genius—they must depend upon a good memory, and this may best be aided by having things written down, which would else escape and be lost.

We should therefore conclude that every man who goes into society, and has an inclination for that kind of conversation, ought to keep some record of the happy trifles he hears upon various occasions. But it seems, at least in Ireland, as if the repugnance to doing this amounted to a conclusive argument against it. It is assumed that as surely as a man has such a store, which he looks up beforehand, so surely will he force the conversation towards his points, or bring them in when irrelevant; and an irrelevant joke is hardly a real joke. I have known, indeed, of a college Don having a note-book of wit in his pocket, and peeping at it under the table to refresh his memory. This was regarded as far the best joke about him, and the laughter before he spoke was always greater than when he had sped his shaft. In actual society it has never occurred to me to meet any one who has sustained a reputation for wit in this way. We think that if the suggestion of the current conversation is not strong enough to bring up a smart point naturally, and without effort, it is better that it should be forgotten or unsaid. Let me add the significant fact, that in spite of endless attempts, no printed collection of jokes has ever attained even a decent position in literature.[1]

So much for wit; the case of humour is slightly different.

Humour

§ 30. If wit be the quick flash, the electric spark, the play of summer lightning which warms the colour of con-

[1] I believe I should mention Dean Ramsay's well-known book as an exception.

versation, humour is the sustained side of the ridiculous, the comic way of looking at things and people, which may be manifested either in comment upon the statements made by others or in narrating one's own experiences. Of course in receiving and commenting upon what is being said, no preparation is possible. It depends altogether upon a mental attitude, which looks out with a smile upon the world, and exposes the ridiculous side of human life not more by irony of comment than by mock approval of social vices, mock indignation at social virtues, seriousness when false comedy is being produced, raillery when false tragedy is being paraded with insincerity or empty bombast. In these and a hundred other ways humour receives and criticises what other people say in a company; and if it be coupled *with kindliness of heart and with tact*, may be regarded as the very highest of conversational virtues.

Analogous to this is the display of humour, not in receiving but in producing ideas in company. The humourist is the only good and effective story-teller; for if he is to monopolise a conversation, and require others to listen to him, it must be by presenting human life under a fresh and piquant aspect—in fact, as a little comedy. Thus the lifelike portrayal of any kind of foible—pomposity, obsequiousness, conceit, hypocrisy, nay even of provincial accent or ungrammatical language—ensures a pleased and therefore agreeable audience, and opens the way for easy and sympathetic intercourse. It is perhaps not too much to say that in any society where conventionality becomes a threatening power, humour is our great safeguard from this kind of vulgarity. Let me point as an illustration of this to the social sketches in *Punch*, which for years back have been the truest mirror of the vulgarities of English society. The humorous exhibition of these foibles is the most effective way we know of bringing them before the public mind, and of warning people that here is a judge whose censure is really to be feared. We may also learn from the success of this extraordinary paper how much more valuable and more respected prepared humour is than prepared wit. The jokes in the text pass by unheeded, while the sketches of character are thought deserving of a permanent place in our literature.

§ 31. I need hardly add that the abuse of these great natural gifts is not only possible, but frequent, and in both it arises from the same mental defects—conceit and selfishness. A man who can say a good thing or make a person appear ridiculous may be so proud of his power that he exercises it at the cost of good taste and even of real humanity. The great wit is often cruel, and even glories in wounding to the quick the sensibilities of others. If he can carry some of the company with him he has a wicked enjoyment in making one of the rest a butt or target for his shafts, and so destroying all wholesome conversation. He may leave in the minds of his society an admiration of his talent, but often a serious dislike of his character. With such feelings abroad he will injure conversation far more than he promotes it. People may consent to go into his company to hear him talk, but will avoid talking in his presence.

The excesses of the humourist are perhaps rather those of a complacent selfishness, which does not hesitate to monopolise the company with long stories in which all do not feel an interest. But humour is its own antidote ; and if a man have the true vein in him he will also have the tact to feel when he is tedious, and when his fun is out of harmony with his hearers. For these reasons it is not only a higher but a safer gift than wit for the purposes of conversation; the pity of it is that so few possess it, and that there is hardly any use in trying to attain it by education. No doubt the constant society of an elder or superior who looks at things in this way may stimulate it in the young, but with the danger of making them sarcastic and satirical, which are grave faults, and which are the distortion of humour to ill-natured and unsocial purposes, so that even in this view of the matter education in humour may turn out a very mischievous failure.

On the whole we must set ourselves to carry on society and to make good conversation without any large help from these brilliant but dangerous gifts. Occasional flashes will occur to ordinary people, and sometimes the very circumstances themselves will create a situation so humorous that it requires no genius to bring it home to the company. But beyond the necessary cautions above indicated, we cannot bring it into any systematic doctrine of social intercourse.

OBJECTIVE CONDITIONS. THE COMPANY —ITS NUMBER

§ 32. We have now exhausted all the conditions which lie in the speaker, which must be brought by him into a society as the subjective conditions of good conversation. Let us turn to the company, regarded as the object with which he is to deal, and see what an analysis of its varieties may teach us in the way of practical direction.

The very first and most obvious division is that of quantity. You may be required to converse either with one person, with a few, or with many. And though no agreeable person may take the trouble to think about it, he nevertheless makes considerable modifications in his talk according to these circumstances. Thus a colloquy with a single person, which is the easiest form, for it is usually with some one who is not a stranger, and it allows far more personality, should consist in a direct interchange of serious opinion, in which each seeks to make the other speak out in confidence his inmost character. You should turn the conversation upon the other person's life, inquire into his or her history, so far as that can be done with good taste and without impertinence, and so induce him (or her) to give personal recollections or confessions, which are to the teller of them generally of the deepest interest. But you will not elicit these without some frankness on your own part, sometimes without volunteering some slight confession which may induce the other to open the flood-gates of his inner life. When this is once attained there must ensue good conversation; for to have a volume of human character laid open before you, and to turn over its pages at leisure, is one of the highest and most intense recreations known to an intelligent mind. Such confessions will hardly ever be made to more than one person at a time, and a sympathetic freedom in encouraging the timid by giving parallel experiences in your own life will often make a silent and reserved person agreeable who could never be induced to speak out in a larger company.

As our manners and customs determine these things, it is not usual to have a long *tête-à-tête* with another person of the same sex without choosing your companion and seeking out the opportunity ; but, on the contrary, two people of different sexes are often brought together and ordered (so to speak) to converse, for no other reason than the command of society. Thus a young man is introduced to a partner at a ball, or a man of soberer age is directed to take a lady down to dinner. Here, though the company is large, the conversation is really of the kind before us—a dialogue between two persons only, of different sexes, and often comparative strangers. There is no case more frequent where conversation is imperative, and where failures are common and conspicuous. It is bad enough to begin with truisms about the weather—an excusable exordium; it is far worse and more disgraceful to end with them, and positively many people get no further. And yet this failure is not from mere emptiness of mind. These very same people, young and old, could be brought into circumstances where almost any of them would be interesting—not a few of them eloquent.

I have spent an evening shut up with a very unpromising commercial traveller in a remote country inn, and yet by trying honestly to find out what he knew and liked, succeeded in drawing from him a most interesting account of his experiences, first in tea-tasting, then in tea-selling to the Irish peasants in the remote glens of Donegal. What he told me was quite worthy to make an article in a good magazine. Yet a more unpromising subject for a long dialogue could hardly be found. He and I had apparently not a single interest in common. But when the right vein was touched one had to supply nothing but assent, or an occasional question; the man flowed on with an almost natural eloquence. People said that others had found him morose and unapproachable. It was certainly their fault. This case is cited as an instance that almost anybody can be made to talk, unless he has determined positively that he will not do so, and is moreover a very obstinate person.

§ 33. In the cases with which we started no such obstinacy exists; the people are really ready to talk, but don't know how. The beginning is evidently the difficulty, and surely here, if anywhere, people who have no natural facility should think out some way of opening the conversation, just as chessplayers have agreed on several formal openings in their game. Nothing is easier than to do this, and to do it in such a general manner as will not be ridiculous. It must always be remembered that the most domestic men and women are often the most difficult to rouse into conversation. Their very virtues in home life have dulled their interests in outer things, and the best of mothers have sometimes forgotten to talk about anything except the education of their children. But it is always better worth probing a sound nature than hearing the ready chatter of idleness. For this reason, some serious topic ought to be the best, even for talking with a stranger, since our conversation errs more frequently through frivolity than through gravity.

But it is not the object of this book to give any special directions. They are only useful when framed by each man and woman for their own private use, and any stock proceeding becomes a mere common-place, and as such contemptible. Yet no intelligent person who thinks over it can fail to make out some general lines to be followed on such occasions, and so thousands of men and women will save themselves from the punishment of a dull and tedious evening beside a person whom they might easily find lively and agreeable.

As there are some people who require to be encouraged by finding out their daily interests, and inquiring into them, so there are others who are only to be excited by the stimulus of opposition, by suggesting some opinion adverse to what they believe or advocate, and so tempting them to a friendly controversy. If you enter such a controversy with perfectly good temper, with a desire to be convinced by good arguments, and no further interest than to bring out the latent fire in the other person, it may produce a very good conversation. But the moment you find the points of difference too strongly accentuated, the moment you perceive the dissatisfaction which is so common in people who are losing ground, or who feel they are making no impression, you should turn the stream into another channel, in which you anticipate at least partial agreement.

Talking with a Few

§ 34. These last remarks are very applicable to the case next before us, when conversation is among a few—say from four to eight people—a form of society the best and most suitable for talk, but which is now rather the exception, from the common habit of crowding our rooms or our tables, and getting rid of social obligations as if they were commercial debts. Indeed many of our young people have so seldom heard a general conversation that they grow up in the belief that their only duty in society will be to talk to one man or woman at a time. So serious are the results of the fashion of large dinner-parties. For really good society no dinner-table should be too large to exclude general conversation, and no couples should sit together who are likely to lapse into private discourse.

It is generally thought the fault of the host or hostess if such an evening turns out a failure;[1] and indeed it is possible to bring one incongruous person into a small company, who will so chill or disturb the rest that conversation languishes. But this case is rare, and the fault usually lies

[1] It is right to add that there are hosts and hostesses so anxious for the good entertainment of their friends that this preoccupation spoils their own enjoyment, and so far defeats the very object they have in view. But people so truly desirous of giving pleasure can hardly avoid being pleasant in a better sense than those who do not feel their responsibilities so acutely.

with the company, none of whom take the trouble to tide over any difficulty, or seek to draw out from those present what they like or want to say. I am now looking at the thing from the point of view of the man or woman who comes in as a guest, and whose duty it is to make the evening, or the period of time during which the company is assembled, pass in a pleasant way. Perhaps it is the practical course to consider the usual form in modern society, that of the small dinner-party, and then apply what is to be said upon it to analogous cases.

In the very forefront there stares us in the face that very awkward period which even the gentle Menander notes as the worst possible for conversation, the short time during which people are assembling, and waiting for the announcement of dinner. If the witty man were not usually a selfish person, who will not exhibit his talent without the reward of full and leisurely appreciation, this is the real moment to show his powers. A brilliant thing said at the very start, which sets people laughing, and makes them forget that they are waiting, may alter the whole complexion of the party, may make the silent and distant people feel themselves drawn into the sympathy of common merriment, and thaw the iciness which so often fetters Anglo-Saxon society. But as this faculty is not given to many, so the average man may content himself with having something ready to tell, and this, if possible, in answer to the usual question expressed or implied: Is there any news this afternoon? There are few days that the daily papers will not afford to the intelligent critic something ridiculous either in style or matter which has escaped the ordinary public; some local event, nay, even some local tragedy, may suggest a topic not worth more than a few moments of attention, which will secure the interest of minds vacant, and perhaps more hungry to be fed than their bodies. Here then, if anywhere in the whole range of conversation, the man or woman who desires to be agreeable may venture to think beforehand, and bring with them something ready, merely as the first kick or starting point to make the evening run smoothly.

§ 35. When the company has settled down to dinner, the first care should be to prevent it breaking into couples, and for that purpose some one opposite should be addressed or some question asked which may evoke answers from various people. Above all, however, the particular guest of the night, or the person best known as a wit or story-teller, should *not* be pressed or challenged at the outset—a sort of vulgarity which makes him either shy or angry at being so manifestly *exploité* by the company, so that he is likely either to turn silent or say some ill-humoured things.

The main advice to be given to women to help them in making such a small company agreeable, is to study politics. A vast number of clever and well-read women exclude themselves from a large part of the serious talk of men by neglecting this engrossing and ever-fruitful topic of conversation. Literature, of course, is a still more various and interesting subject; but here perhaps the defect lies with men, who are so devoted to practical life that they lose their taste for general reading. Except for politics, the daily papers seldom afford any literary food fit for good conversation:

The topic which ought to be common to both and always interesting, is the discussion of human character and human motives. If the novel be so popular a form of literature, how can the novel in real life fail to interest an intelligent company? People of serious temper and philosophic habit will be able to confine themselves to large ethical views, and the general dealings of men; but to average people, both men and women, and perhaps most of all to busy men, who desire to find in society relaxation from their toil, that lighter and more personal kind of criticism on human affairs will prevail which is known as *gossip*.

§ 36. This may, therefore, be the suitable moment to consider the place of gossip in the theory of conversation; for though gossip is not only possible but usual in the private discourse of two people, and possible too in a large society, its real home and natural exercising ground is the society of a few people intimate with the same surroundings.

It is usual for all people, especially those who most indulge in it, to censure gossip as a crime, as a violation of the Ninth Commandment, as a proof of idleness and vain curiosity, as a frivolous waste of the time given us for mental improvement. Yet the censure is seldom serious. These people cannot but feel obscurely what they are either afraid to speak out or have not duly considered, that the main object of conversation is neither instruction nor moral improvement but *recreation*. It is of course highly desirable that all our amusements should be both intellectually and morally profitable, and we may look back with special satisfaction upon any conversation which included these important objects. But the main and direct object is recreation, mental relaxation, happy idleness; and from this point of view it is impossible for any sound theory of conversation to ignore or depreciate gossip, which is perhaps the main factor in agreeable talk throughout society.

The most harmless form is the repeating of small details about personages great either in position or intellect, which give their empty names a personal colour, and so bring them nearer and more clearly into view. The man who has just come from the society of kings and queens, or great generals, or politicians, or literary men whose names are exceptionally prominent at the time, can generally furnish some personal details by which people imagine they can explain to themselves great and unexpected results. Who has not heard with interest such anecdotes about Mr. Gladstone, or Prince Bismarck, or Victor Emanuel? And what book has ever acquired more deserved and lasting reputation than Boswell's *Life of Johnson?*

The latest development of the literary side of gossip is to be seen in what are called the 'society papers,' which owe their circulation to their usefulness in furnishing topics for this kind of conversation.[1]

[1] I only speak of the *fact* that they are useful in supply-

All the funny sketches of life and character which have made *Punch* so admirable a mirror of society for the last fifty years, are of the character of gossip, subtracting the mischievous element of personality; and though most people will think this latter an essential feature in our meaning when we talk of gossip, it is not so; it is the trivial and passing, the unproven and suspected, which is the main thing, for it is quite possible to bring any story under the notion while suppressing the names of the actors.

Next to the retailing of small personal points about great people comes the narrating of deeper interests belonging to small people, especially the affairs of the heart, which we pursue so assiduously even in feigned characters. But here it is that all the foibles of our neighbours come under survey, and that a great deal

ing a want. Whether they are or are not corrupting the public mind is another and a very serious question.

of calumny and slander may be launched upon the world by mere shrug and innuendo. The reader will remember with what effect this side of gossip is brought out in Sheridan's *School for Scandal.*

§ 37. It is idle to deny that there is no kind of conversation more fascinating than this, but its immorality may easily become such as to shock honest minds, and the man who indulges in it freely at the expense of others, will probably have to pay the cost himself in the long run; for those who hear him will fear him, and will retire into themselves in his presence. On the other hand, nothing is more honourable than to stand forth as the defender or the palliator of the faults imputed to others, and nothing is easier than to expand such a defence into general considerations as to the purity of human motives, which will raise the conversation from its unwholesome ground into the upper air.

If the company be fit for it, no general rule is more valuable than that of turning the conversation away from people and fixing it on things; but, alas! how many there are who only take interest in people, and in the weakest and most trivial aspects of people! Few things are more essential and more neglected in the education of children than to habituate them to talk about things, and not people; yet, what use is there in urging these more special rules, when the very idea of teaching them to converse at all is foreign to the minds of most parents and of all educators? Let me illustrate this by one grotesque fact.

It will be conceded that the one thing absolutely essential to the education of a lady is that she should talk agreeably at meals. It is the natural meeting time, not only of the household, but of friends, and conversation is then as essential as food. Yet, what is the habit of many of our schools? They either enforce silence at this period, or they compel the wretched pupils to speak in a foreign language, in which they can only labour out spasmodic commonplaces, without any interchange or play of thought. Consequently many of our girls drift into the habit of regarding meal-times as the precise occasion when conversation is impossible. How far this mis-education, during some of the most critical years of their lives, affects them permanently it is not easy to overestimate. If parents were decently intelligent in this matter they should ascertain clearly the practice of a school, and the schoolmaster or schoolmistress who is obtuse and mischievous enough to practise this crime should at once lose every pupil.

The only excuse I can find for this widespread outrage upon the social rights of the young, is the old tradition of universities, still pursued in convent schools and Roman Catholic seminaries, that a portion of scripture, or of some edifying book, should be read out during meals, so that the pupils may take in spiritual food along with their dinners, and avoid the crime of light and trivial conversation. A clever Jesuit educator whom I knew, went so far within the letter of the law as to substitute the *Saturday Review* for the usual work of edification, the *Lives of the Saints!* This worthy man did his best under a system devised to bring up young people in silence and in fear, not in free and friendly intercourse with their instructors. But why should we, with our spiritual liberty, retain these mischievous and antiquated shackles?

With Many

§ 38. Conversation with a crowd, or even with a large number of people, is almost a contradiction in terms. How can there be interchange of thought or repartee where so many clashing fancies make confusion rather than harmony? In ordinary society, therefore, it is the obvious solution to break up a large company into couples or small groups, and so reduce this case to one of the preceding. Two exceptional forms may be noted, which come, perhaps, upon the verge of conversation proper: the one where a good story-teller, or person who has had some wonderful experience, is ready to talk for the benefit of the whole company, and receive occasional support from questions put to him by various people. But even in this case the number must be limited, and usually such a talker will seem to his audience egotistical, for people who want to have their little private say, and tell their little modest story, feel ousted by the monopoly of the leading spirit.

Perhaps the pleasantest form into which to lead such a conversation, is a sort of public dialogue, in which one or two querists will draw from the real object of attention his views, or question his statements in such a way as to provoke the exercise of his powers. This is the kind of conversation to be found in Plato's *Dialogues*, which are quite fitted for a large company, though but few speakers share in them. But I will not be bound to admire these immortal compositions as specimens of conversation. To the modern reader, they cease to be such as soon as they become serious, and I may even venture to say that in any modern society they would justly be voted tedious.

§ 39. The second case worth noticing here is when a leading person, king or viceroy, or princess, or political magnate, entertains a crowd of people mostly inferior in station, and has to perform the duty of going through the rooms and talking in succession to all sorts and conditions of men. If on the one hand the people addressed are sure to be flattered by such attention, and therefore responsive and anxious to be pleased, on the other there is no social duty which gives more scope for all the mental and moral perfections already enumerated, and therefore there is no more certain test of conversational ability. For here the talk is not really with many at a time, nor again is it the conversation with one person, in which the main element is the sustaining of interest for a considerable time; it is a series of brief successive dialogues, in which the two great difficulties of conversation, the starting of it and the breaking off, are perpetually recurring. The speaker is even debarred from the use of any fixed formula or method of overcoming these difficulties, for the people addressed will be sure to compare notes, and will reject as insincere any politenesses which are administered according to a formula, however graceful it may appear.

Here then, if anywhere, the art must consist in concealing the art. But let none imagine that art has no place here. A sympathetic nature, which readily apprehends the interests of other minds, is not more useful to the great man or woman than a careful previous study of the company, who they are, what they have done, what the distinction or the hobby of each of them may be. Nothing is easier than to acquire such information from the staff whose duty is to furnish it. A great natural aptitude or a specially trained memory is required to remember the various scraps of information about each, and to fit them to the proper names. It is said that royal personages often inherit an exceptional power of remembering names and persons from the exercise of this faculty by a long line of successive ancestors. But the suggestion of an equerry or a lord-in-waiting is in such cases the usual and more obvious cause of this apparent genius, which the flattery of courtiers exaggerates with shameless effrontery.

However this may be, the knowledge, inspired or acquired, of the name and circumstances of an inferior is the great key to smoothing over the difficulty of beginning a conversation, for any personal question will be taken as a compliment, and evidence of a friendly interest on the part of the prince. The breaking off with ease and grace is more difficult, for I do not count the formal bow of dismissal or the prearranged interruption by a new presentation as more than awkward subterfuges. Some form of expressing regret that the moment does not admit of fuller discussion of the subject already commenced, and a hope to resume it, is of course an obvious and polite way of closing the interview, or a question as to some one else who must receive attention, or a complaint that duty must oust pleasure—

there are myriad possibilities, as may be seen from the conversation of the few great ladies in England who have the gift or have attained the art. I mention ladies because the traditional bluntness and simplicity inherited, respected, assumed, affected by most Englishmen makes them very averse to this social grace. It is no accident that those of our great houses who have adopted public life after a considerable experience of French manners, and with a ready knowledge of the French language, are the most brilliant exceptions. Perhaps, too, Irish vivacity has in most of these cases added life and brightness to their talk. But, as a rule, it is to women that we look for this talent, and to older French society for the best examples of it. One often hears it said that since Lady Waldegrave's death no one in London knows how to have a *salon*. This, whether true or false, is the popular recognition of that social excellence in conversing with many, to which I have devoted the last few pages.

The Quality of the Company

§ 40. Hitherto we have regarded the company merely from the point of quantity, and considered them as so many units, grouped in larger and smaller masses. We shall now adopt a totally different principle, and regard their *quality* in relation to the speaker. It is obvious that for our purpose this element must receive careful consideration.

I remember years ago occupying myself in constructing from the epitaphs in a country church the genealogy of the great squire who owned the parish. Among the stereotyped and hardly varied eulogies of his ancestors one stood out as peculiar and original. It was said of this magnate, who died about the year 1830, that to express his virtues among those that knew him would be impertinent, 'but to strangers and to posterity let this monument declare, that in him were combined *the generous Patron*, *the affable Superior*, *the polished Equal*, the uncompromising Patriot, and the Honest Man.' The sequel was commonplace. Nor is the social description complete, for the dignity of the subject would not allow the epitaphist to suggest the virtues of his hero in the guise of an inferior. *The supple courtier* would, from what I have heard about him, have been the truest addition to the picture. But what interests us here is not only the importance given to social talents over morals and religion,—a truly Irish feature,—but the accurate perception the writer had of the various talents required according to the quality of the people around us.

If he had thought more upon the subject, or if he had been allowed to give us the results of his thinking, he might have told us that the secret in all cases, and the *sine qua non* of good conversation, is to establish equality, at least momentary, if you like fictitious, but at all costs *equality*, among the members of the company who make up the party. The man who keeps asserting his superiority, or confessing his inferiority, is never agreeable. Nay even, if the superiority is very marked, as in the case of royal persons, it is almost impossible to converse with them in the better sense, and one of the most melancholy penalties of this kind of greatness is, that except within the narrow circle of their families and equals they can never enjoy the fresh breeze of unconstrained society. Any truth they can learn from their surroundings is confined to the very poor category of pleasant truths. All vigorous intellectual buffeting, all wholesome contradiction which would open their minds, is carefully avoided by courtiers, because it is the assertion of this very equality which is the backbone of conversation. It requires peculiar earnestness and honesty on the part of a prince to break through this crust of assentation, and discover the real opinions of the men around him; nor can he incur any bitterer loss than the removal of those rare advisers, who have the gift of combining real liberty with formal obsequiousness, and without violating the etiquette of the courtier, can assume the character of the independent critic and just adviser.

But this little book is not meant for the advice or criticism of kings, who by their position are almost completely excluded from conversation. The question before us is how we ordinary people should modify the tone of our talk according as our company consists of people socially or intellectually above us, of our equals, or lastly, of our inferiors. It is evident that in the first and last cases there is difficulty; the second is the normal atmosphere of conversation.

TALKING WITH SUPERIORS

§ 41. In conversing with superiors, we must broadly distinguish the socially from the intellectually superior. For the art of producing agreeable society in the former case differs widely from doing so in the latter. Perhaps the matter may be expressed tersely, if not quite accurately, by saying that the necessary equality between the members of the company is attained in the former instance by the good talker raising himself to the level of his superior, in the latter by his bringing down his superior to his own level. A word of explanation is here necessary. The man or woman that succeeds among social superiors is not the timid or modest person, afraid to contradict, and ever ready to assent to what is said, but rather the free and independent intellect that suggests subjects, makes bold criticisms, and in fact introduces a bright and free tone into a company which is perhaps somewhat dull from its grandeur or even its extreme respectability. It is a case of the socially superior acknowledging another kind of superiority, which redresses the balance. We need hardly add that the greatest stress must here be placed on tact, for to presume on either kind of superiority will cause offence, and so spoil every attempt at breaking the bonds set around us by the grades of the social hierarchy.

If, on the contrary, we meet a man of acknowledged mental superiority, whether generally or in his special department, it is our social duty by intelligent questioning, by an anxiety to learn from him, to force him to condescend to our ignorance, or join in our fun, till his broader sympathies are awakened, and he plays with us as if we were his children. Indeed this very metaphor points out one of the very remarkable instances of social equality asserted by an inferior—I mean the outspoken freedom of the child—which possesses a peculiar charm, and often thaws the dignity or dissipates the reserve of the great man and woman whose superiority is a perpetual obstacle to them in ordinary society.

I may here dwell a moment upon conscious superiority and its companion, that conscious inferiority which is the great social barrier to conversation, and which in most cases actually prohibits all intercourse. In other European countries the separation of *noblesse* and *bourgeoisie* is carried so far as wellnigh to annihilate all free and intellectual society of the better kind. The intellectually-educated classes are so thoroughly excluded from social education in the urbanity and grace of noble society, that they sink into mere intellectual boors, while the aristocrats so seldom hear any intellectual discussion or take any interest in learning, that their society becomes either vapidly trivial or professionally narrow. For these nobles have their professions like other people, especially the profession of arms.

The case is not so bad among us, where there are always great commoners, where eminent success in making money, or even in letters, brings men and women into the highest society, and where there are some of the greatest positions in the country from which our Peers are even excluded. There is no doubt that an intellectual man, or a man of strong and recognised character, whatever his origin, can easily take a place in high society among us. But how many lesser people are there of excellent social gifts who assume most falsely that they are not suited, and will not be welcome, to the higher classes, and so avoid both the pleasure and the profit to be derived from a more refined, though not more cultivated, stratum than their own! I am here talking of really modest and worthy people, not of those vain and vulgar persons who make it a boast—often a very dishonest one—that they have spurned associating with their superiors, from a profound contempt of what they call *toadyism*.

§ 42. This term, which expresses the vicious relations of socially inferior and superior, is used in very vague senses, ranging from a just censure of meanness in others to a mistaken assertion of independence in ourselves. Nothing is more inherent in all European society derived from the feudal and ecclesiastical traditions of the Middle Ages—probably in every cultivated society—than to honour rank and social dignity as such, apart from the real worth of the person so distinguished. This is the basis of that loyalty to sovrans which even when irrational does not incur the imputation of toadyism. People of independent rank and personal dignity even still accept and prize semi-menial offices about a Court, without losing either respect among ordinary people or even self-respect.

There is then such a thing as respect for rank as such, and a feeling of pride in the contact with it, which is regarded as honourable. When does the virtue of loyalty pass into a vice? Clearly when the higher and more important duties of life are postponed to this love of outward dignity. The man who neglects his equals for the purpose of courting his superiors, still more who confesses or asserts his inferiority when associating with them, and who submits to rebuffs and indignities for the sake of being thought their associate, above all, who condones in them vices which he would not brook in an equal, is justly liable to the charge, which, however, only asserts the exaggeration of a tendency affecting almost all his censors.

The usual thing, however, is to hear

people censured for the *fact* of associating with those above them, as if this were in itself a crime. There is, too, not unfrequently an element of jealousy in our criticism, and of secret regret that another has attained certain advantages, or supposed advantages, to which we ourselves feel an equal claim. Yet one thing is certain, that if the supposed toady exhibited in the society which he courts the qualities ascribed to him by his critics, he would very soon lose his position and miss the very object of his ambition. The only cause of his popularity is the very fact that his company feel him in some respects their equal, possibly their superior, and it is the secret of asserting this equality with tact and courtesy which makes men and women popular among their superiors.

There is one point of view which gives a good talker a distinct advantage under these circumstances. The distinctness of his ordinary associates from those whom he occasionally meets makes his everyday experience different from theirs, and so things familiar to him and his everyday society are often interesting and novel to people of a different standing. He ought therefore to be able to bring new information to bear upon either class of society, and so secure its interest with his store of fresh experiences.

WITH INFERIORS

§ 43. Let us now turn to the other side and consider the proper principles of conversation with inferiors. And here, too, it is more practical to take our standpoint in the middle class of society, and not among those who must habitually talk to inferiors owing to their own high condition. The same key unlocks the secret of success. If it be indispensable for good conversation to make your superiors feel you for the time their equal, so it is indispensable that your inferiors should feel that they too are upon a social level with you during their talk. Of course, the first thing is to banish all traces of *condescension*, that odious ape of humility and urbanity, which is the loud expression of want of brains and want of tact, for it emphasises the very differences which conversation seeks to obliterate. On the other hand, there is an extreme of *familiarity* which shocks and alarms the inferior, for he justly expects a sudden revulsion from it, as we are told in Polybius of the common people of Antioch, into whose humble entertainments or amusements Antiochus Epiphanes would come, and sit down to drink and joke with them. These vagaries on the part of their despotic sovran so frightened them that they would get up and run away. The just mean is to strike out a line of conversation, either of common interest, or in which the inferior is a specialist, and therefore your superior. He will then feel that he is speaking with authority, and the honest expression of your ignorance and your desire to learn will give him confidence to tell you freely what he knows.

§ 44. It is in the lower ranks of society that national differences become really great. The highly bred or highly cultivated people of any European nation have attained a certain unity of type, and are interested by the same sort of conversation; it is very different with English, French, Italian, and German peasants. Nay, even within our islands, there is a marked difference in the social abilities of English, Scotch, and Irish peasants. It is customary to set this down to race, and be satisfied with some such vague generality. But I fancy the causes of these social differences are rather recent than primeval; they do not depend directly upon climate or atmosphere, and if I may quote the opinion of a wise friend on this large question, I should say that one chief cause of the talking or social ability of some peasantries over others is the fact that their proximate ancestors were a bilingual people. Thus the great majority of West Irish and North Scotch peasants are descended from grandfathers, whose talk oscillated between Celtic and English, and who were therefore constantly educated in intelligence by the problem of *translating* ideas from one language into another, not to mention the distinct inheritance of the special ideas peculiar to each and every language. This is an education in expression, in thinking, and therefore in conversation, wholly foreign to the English Midland boor, who has never heard more than two or three hundred words of a very rude provincial dialect of English, and therefore commands neither the words nor the ideas of the outlying provinces. A great part of the French peasantry are likewise proximately descended from bilingual ancestors, French being the old language of but a small part of their now recognised territory. Breton, Bearnais, Provençal, Walloon, are even still living languages in large parts of France (as was German up to 1871), and so the peasantry were under like favourable conditions.

But I must not diverge further from the subject in hand. Thus much was naturally suggested to me by the best and most diverting conversation I know with inferiors—that which sporting men have with those whose livelihood has been earned by studying the habits and ways of fish and game. There are few men who shoot, fish, or hunt in Ireland, who do not know specimens of that remarkable though small class whose natural ability, combined with long experience, makes them masters of their craft, and whose long association with their superiors in matters of sport has given them perfect ease and even charm of manners. Conversation with these people, which is often prolonged through many hours, is not only very instructive—a secondary matter to us now—but exceedingly amusing, from the perfect frankness as well as tact with which they speak their mind to the sporting friend, whom they regard as their inferior or equal from a professional point of view. It is this perfect liberty, this spiritual equality, often designated as the free masonry of sport, from which arises the charm of talking upon subjects of common interest to one confessedly inferior in many respects. But in one he is commonly your superior, even apart from his sport. It has been far more important to him all his life to study and know the characters of his employers than it has been for them to study his, and so he is generally your superior in perceiving what will please, and what topics are to be selected or avoided in conversation. Nothing has struck me more in many such talks than the acute estimate which these people form of the strength and weakness of those who are their patrons.

These are illustrations of a general kind, to show how inferiority in social station may not imply inferiority for the purposes of conversation, so that we may even here attain that equality which I regard as essential for its success.

THE RELATIONS OF SEX AND AGE

§ 45. So far we have been considering the quality of the company as determined by social position, which, if not an absolutely artificial distinction, is at least frequently such, so that it may be even reversed by circumstances. There are great distinctions made by nature which are indelible, and which must therefore be reckoned with as permanent factors in our theory—I mean those of age and sex.

There are, properly speaking, three grades of age worth considering—youth, maturity, and old age; but from our point of view we are justified in regarding mature life as the normal state, and shall therefore consider the duties of the mature man and woman as they come in contact with the extremes. It is not worth while writing any advices for the old, as they are beyond the age of improvement, though by no means always stripped of their social qualities; indeed, the position of very old people, who have maintained their faculties, is quite exceptional in modern society, and will require a few words of comment in the present connection.

A collection of very old people is of

course hardly to be found; so that the practical case before us is the occurrence of one, or at most two, very old people in a company, and the consequent modifications in ordinary society likely to make this element effective and agreeable. It may almost be assumed that however lively the old person is, he (or she) will not be able to converse when many people are talking in the room, and to assert himself in even a small crowd. There must be comparative silence while he is speaking, and special attention should be paid him. Under these circumstances it almost follows as a matter of course that he should be discreetly drawn out to tell such experiences as are beyond the memory of the rest, which from their pictures of bygone manners or long dead celebrities are very interesting, and admirably suited for the best social recreation. The many *Recollections*, *Diaries*, *Autobiographies*, etc., now published from the papers of the mere observers of their age, such as Greville, and which are generally too trivial and minute to make good books, form the staple of excellent conversation when told by the very actor or observer. Of course there is a considerable chance of his becoming tedious; it is one of the most frequent defects of age, but if a man's hobby makes him tedious, it also may make him very interesting; and the first and best receipt to make a man agreeable is to make him talk about what he likes best.

The most successful conversations with old men are, however, not those with the old *raconteur*, who is in the habit of narrating his experiences and expects to be asked to do so, but with some modest and apparently dull old person who is successfully probed by intelligent and sympathetic questions, till he is actually reminded of long-forgotten scenes, which have perhaps not been suggested to him for years, and then he draws from his memory, with the help of further questions, some passage of life and adventure of the highest interest. Many a time have I seen an old person, at first regarded as an obstacle, prove the highest advantage to the conversation, and it is for this reason that in a book of theory the reader should be reminded of his duty to see that so valuable an item does not escape him. It is generally easy enough to gather from the old gentleman (or lady) where he has lived, what society he has frequented, and what are his strongest impressions as to the contrasts between his own early days and ours.

There is, moreover, in discussing the gossip and the scandal of a bygone generation an amount of freedom—I had almost said licence—allowed which would be intolerable as regards living society, and a very old person may be allowed to say things which younger people should avoid. I do not mention this as an advantage in itself—far from it—but as an additional possibility in making conversation lively, and in avoiding that stagnation in talk which, from our present point of view, is the extremest crime known to society.

It is also obvious that as old people are unable to talk loudly and with vivacity, the dialogue between two, or a couple of listeners added to the questioner, will be the most likely way to attain the end in view. To stop an old person who is becoming tedious is probably the most difficult of all social duties, and requires the most delicate tact. The respect due to age takes from our hands those weapons of sarcasm, banter, or even blunt interruption which are our natural defences against obtrusive youth; nor do I know of any general directions which can help a host or hostess in this grave and not uncommon difficulty. It is of course useless to lecture old people, either in this book or elsewhere, on the dangers of tediousness.

§ 46. I turn now to conversation with people much younger than ourselves, not of course with babies, or very young children, the art of amusing whom can hardly be called the art of conversation. I mean rather such ordinary cases as going in to dinner with a person much younger than yourself, whose main interests must therefore be foreign to yours; or else the entertaining of a party of young people who have met for purposes of sport, but are also to be regarded as guests at a table where conversation asserts its universal importance.

What modifications in our talk are here desirable?

In the first place it is but natural that the older person should lead the discourse, and suggest the topics which will elicit sympathy from the young. And of course the easiest way to begin is to make people talk about themselves—this being a subject which interests most young people exceedingly. But it is by no means an universal rule. The life of the young, of schoolboys, and of young girls, is often very monotonous, and really affords no scope for conversation beyond the first ordinary inquiries into their tastes, habits, and what they read. If you find a strong taste for any special thing, such as music or cricket, you may work out that subject.

But if, as is too often the case, the youth has not thought seriously about anything, it is surely best to draw from your own stores, and tell experiences which will be new and interesting from their curiosity, such as the ways and habits of the lower animals which you may have observed, the manners of men, or of strange cities which you have visited, the feats you have seen performed. These things are seldom suitable for other kinds of society, when any display of your own experiences is offensive; but in talking to young, fresh, and ingenuous people, the novelty of the information you give them will generally obscure their critical or fault-finding sense, and even if they are very sceptical as to facts,—the young and inexperienced in our day are usually so,—they will fully appreciate the effort to make them feel happy.

§ 47. It is perhaps not till then that you will succeed in probing out some interesting nook in their short experience. They have been in accidental contact with some great or notorious person, and have seen him in his leisure moments; they may have lived in a peculiar country, where either the sport or the natural features are very interesting, and upon which they can have the distinction of instructing older and wiser people.

I have met quiet country gentlemen,

who in their youth had seen active service in the army, and fought in remarkable campaigns, who never spoke of these things among their neighbours, so that when some intelligent stranger drew from them their experiences, it came like a revelation to those who for years had voted them stupid and dull members of their county society.

So important and so neglected is this duty of probing for the strong point of others, which is naturally brought forward in connection with the effort to talk with the young and inexperienced, that I am disposed to lay this down as a practical rule: *if you find the company dull, blame yourself.* With more skill and more patience on your part it is almost certain you would have found it agreeable. If even two or three people in a company acted on this rule, how seldom would our social meetings prove a failure!

§ 48. We come now to a still more indelible contrast than that of age, and ask what effects, advantageous or otherwise, has the contrast of sex upon conversation? It is a problem very difficult indeed to solve, for while it is a great law of nature that the very instincts of each sex urge it to please the other, it is on the contrary a great law of society that (perhaps for this very reason) a large number of topics are not to be discussed by the sexes in common. It is then a case where nature stimulates and tradition restrains: which shall we declare to be stronger? That depends altogether upon the character of the society in which we live. If it be perfectly free—let us say the society of the Navigator Islands—there the natural attraction of opposite sexes must make their conversation far more agreeable than that of men or women separately.

So it is too among those exceptional sets of people in civilised countries, who brave public opinion so far as to speak their minds to the other sex, and whose conversation is accordingly considered too free by the average of people around them. In this it is natural that the more restrained sex should take the initiative; but if any woman makes bold to speak with perfect freedom among men, and if she be gifted with the ordinary talents for conversation, she will be more agreeable than an intelligent man who says the same things—or rather she will say things in a fresher way; the very situation is somewhat piquant, and so she will certainly gain by the contrast of sex. A small party of men and women of this sort ought to produce the most amusing conversation possible. But I need only hint how easily such a society may transgress the due limits, and degenerate into what the later Athenians thought brilliant, and collected in a special book. Nor will freedom, far less audacity, in conversation redeem ignorance, rudeness, or graver vices.

Take another kind of society, either one of Puritanical strictness—I remember when the word *girl* was thought rather improper in religious Dublin society, you should say *young person*—or else that sort of foreign society which, from suspicion and fear, prohibits any intimacy between young men and women, or brands such intimacy as foreign to good society. There can be no doubt that here contrast of sex is fatal to conversation, which must needs be constrained, conventional, and occupied with topics either too trivial or too serious for proper recreation. Women living under these conditions find no interest in studying the subjects that interest men—especially politics; and so it comes to pass that in the greater part of orderly modern English society, a company of men only is thought more agreeable than a mixed one—even though the ladies be not so strict as in the extreme cases mentioned, but merely confined to domestic and moral topics, to the exclusion of public affairs.

§ 49. This being the general aspect of the problem, it only remains to apply the principles already attained in the case of a dialogue with one of the other sex. In old times, that extreme form of courtesy called gallantry was thought the proper way to please a woman. It is now almost vulgar, and the man who desires to flatter an intelligent woman most keenly, and interest her, will take care to treat her as an intellectual equal, not as a plaything or a pet. A man who seizes the opportunity of a conversation to consult a lady on some social difficulty, or makes her for the moment his confidante in some matter not to be divulged, will be almost sure to find her agreeable and sympathetic.

Men, especially elderly men, are far more easily flattered by women, and more easily carried away by such flattery. For this reason I think it unnecessary, nay, perhaps mischievous, to give any advices to ladies how to use this powerful engine in society. The real difficulty under which they labour as to conversation is to hit off the right mean between prudery and its opposite, to know how far to speak out frankly, and when to put a bridle on the talker who threatens to overstep the bounds of the reverence due to ourselves and to one another.

This reverence is, of course, due most especially to youth, and elderly people who discuss before young boys and girls any topics not perfectly pure, are guilty of such a crime in conversation as can hardly be punished too severely. Before other elderly people the case is somewhat different, and things may then be said or implied which should not be selected for discussion in the presence of the young. But above all, let us be strict in checking this kind of licence, which is so apt to take possession of the baser minds among us, and degrade conversation—the recreation of intellect and the mirror of social goodness—into a serious mischief.

§ 50. What I have said above concerning the duty of treating the other sex as strict equals in conversation, is but another instance of the principle already laid down (§ 40), that no really bright social intercourse is possible without equality. There is, in fact, nothing so democratic as good conversation, nothing so Protestant, for we must seem to assert our private judgment, even where we assent. And as a man does best to seek a woman's opinion, and ask her advice, so as to make her feel on the same plane, a woman who desires to be agreeable should differ without hesitation from the opinions expressed by men, and assert her independence of judgment, and her consequent right to take part in a real conversation. A woman who does this, even stupidly, and without good reasons, is better than those who sit down and acquiesce in whatever is said by men; this latter is the acknowledgment of inferiority which is subversive of all pleasant talk.

Degrees of Intimacy

§ 51. The only other classification of the members of a small society worth making here is in accordance with the various degrees of their previous intimacy. They may either be a family party consisting of near relations, or a friendly party consisting of intimate friends, or a party of casual acquaintances who meet not unfrequently, or a chance collection of almost strangers. In all these cases there is naturally some modification to be made in the rules and conditions of agreeable talking. And first of all let us warn those who think it is not worth while taking trouble to talk in their family circle, or who read the newspaper at meals, that they are making a mistake which has far-reaching consequences. It is nearly as bad as those convent schools or ladies' academies, when either silence or a foreign tongue is imposed at meals, and concerning which I have already spoken. Whatever people may think of the value of theory, there is no doubt whatever that practice is necessary for conversation, and it is at home, among those who are intimate, and free in expressing their thoughts, that this practice must be sought. It is thus, and thus only, that young people can go out into the world properly provided with the only universal introduction to society—agreeable manners.

Here, then, conversation is not so much a recreation as a duty, and so becomes too grave a matter for this book. I will merely say a word upon the position of a guest who is introduced into such a party, to whose daily trifles, family feuds, or friendships, he is a stranger. It is of course the first duty of the family not to monopolise the topics by discussing family histories unknown and uninteresting beyond their circle. Menander long ago complained of the misfortune of falling into a party of this kind.[1] On the other hand, the stranger must assume a temporary interest in affairs outside his ordinary life, and merely for the sake of his hosts. But if he is appealed to as an umpire by members who habitually differ in opinion (and this he will easily note), let him be very wary of giving a decision, and rather discover that there is truth on each side of the question.

§ 52. Far easier is the position of a party of intimate friends. They have probably become friends simply because

[1] Cf. my *Social Life of Greece*, p. 317.

they enjoy each other's society, and have many topics of interest in common. It requires no exertion to make them talk, and they will readily condone moments of taciturnity and depression in one or more members of the party. They want no advice, and need no instruction, for this is the only true and permanent human bond which makes men and women ever sympathetic, and ever agreeable to one another.

§ 53. As regards a company of strangers, on the contrary, all the principles stated in the earlier parts of this book will have their clearest application. To interest or to fascinate a stranger requires all the gifts there enumerated, and in proportion as we possess them, and take pains to use them, we shall succeed in turning the stranger into the friend. There is no greater test of conversational powers than to go into a company of strangers, to make them feel at home, to turn their minds to some common thought, and establish an agreeable and sociable spirit where there was at first nothing but coldness and diffidence. To do this single handed is a feat beyond the power of most people. But if several persons make an effort in the same direction, the combination will effect what a single genius can hardly accomplish.

Nothing proves more conclusively the value of practice in these things than the fact that the higher classes, who are compelled through constant moving about both at home and abroad to converse frequently with casual acquaintances, and who in various society often meet strangers—these are the people in whom we generally observe ease in conversation under such conditions. We set it down to good breeding, but this means that not only they but their ancestors have been practising it. Hereditary virtues have not been created with less labour than any other virtues. Generally they require the efforts of several generations, and are therefore the most arduous and meritorious of all.

The Topics of Conversation—Serious and Trivial

§ 54. Having now exhausted the subjective side, that is to say the qualities in the speaker and the conditions among the hearers which make or mar conversation, it is natural to proceed to the objective side and see how far we can classify the topics which form the matter of our talk. Of course a division of the actual subjects under specific heads would require an encyclopædia, and even then would never be complete, for the very essence of good conversation is to wander through all possible things in heaven, in earth, and under the earth without bond or limit, the only universal condition being that we should range far and near and seek all possible variety, or rather let ourselves drift from point to point, and not determine to hold a fixed course. The quantity, therefore, of subjects being infinite, and so not to be described, we must content ourselves with regarding them in quality as either serious or trivial; in relation to the speakers, as either universal or personal; in the mode of treatment, as handled either in council, in controversy, or in exposition.

§ 55. Our theory has declared itself long ago against over-seriousness in conversation. This caution is specially necessary nowadays,—when people read so many books and work so hard,—lest they should regard conversation as a deliberate method of instruction and channel of improvement. Nay, these very objects will be far better attained indirectly and by the way, while the company is indulging in talk as a recreation.

But it is almost needless to say that the most solid and lasting recreation, the most excellent refreshment of the soul, is to be had from very serious converse, especially where not more than two or three are gathered together, and to exclude this precious comfort from any theory of conversation would be absurd. On the other hand, when two people are earnestly engaged on a really serious topic, we may leave them to themselves, and need not intrude upon them any idle considerations as to their manner of treating it. For this is not conversation in the proper sense. 'In this frame of mind,' says Hawthorne in his *Transformation* (chap. ii.), 'men sometimes find their profoundest truths side by side with the idlest jest, and utter one or the other, apparently without distinguishing which is the more valuable or assigning any considerable value to either.' He hits the truth exactly. Great seriousness is as detrimental to a general talk as excessive trifling. For as the latter fails after a few moments to interest people who have any sense, so the former fails to recreate or amuse, and is in fact earnest work invading the proper domain of leisure.

There is therefore no general direction here possible save to avoid both extremes, or rather to avoid persistence in either extreme, for it is better to have them in turn, than to cultivate subjects which are indifferent. Brilliant talk should alternate between grave and gay, and above all shun dryness, detail, minuteness—in a word, tediousness.

The moment at which by common consent people talk trivialities is the moment of first introduction. And here the weather is almost invariably the first pawn to be moved. It is amazing what triteness and endless repetition is tolerated by society on this point. The facts stated are common property, and agreed to by all, so that the first object of ordinary people seems to be to express nothing while they are saying something. Yet I suppose what is sanctioned by almost universal practice must have some good reason behind it, and is perhaps meant to give people time to observe each other without apparent rudeness. This method of opening the game seems, however, so stale that every sensible person should have some paradox or heresy about the weather ready whereby he may break through this idle skirmishing and make the people about him begin to think as soon as possible. On the other hand it is easy to overdo this attempt, and begin with something so serious that the unprepared audience is frightened and chilled. Thus there can be no greater blunder than to inquire suddenly about the state of a man's soul, a sort of *coup* which many pious people have actually thought a decent introduction to a conversation.

THE TOPICS OF CONVERSATION—GENERAL AND PERSONAL

§ 56. Here we have before us one of the most difficult of problems, and which I shall rather state than attempt to solve. Should we aim at making our conversation universal in subject, or should we prefer it to be on personal topics, such as gossip or scandal—the character of some mutual friend, an enemy, and so forth? There is not the smallest doubt that if we wish it to be profitable and improving, personal topics should be avoided, and that we should talk not about people but about things. And when an assembly of really cultivated people discusses literary questions, such as the comparative merits of poets or novelists, there is not only great pleasure to be gained from such a society, but the after-taste is good, and you feel that your leisure has not been in vain.

On the other hand it is idle to deny that in most companies people have not read or thought enough to join in such a conversation or to enjoy it, whereas details of personal life, the latest anecdote, the facts or surmises about some scandal, the adverse criticism of some acquaintance—all this kind of thing, ranging from harmless gossip into libellous scandal, is deeply interesting to almost everybody, and though by no means improving is always entertaining.

But even so let the scandalmonger beware. If his ordinary topics are the characters of his acquaintances, he will soon find himself shunned or treated with suspicion by society; and nothing so completely kills all the pleasure of a company as a protest from any one present that he will not have his absent friend maligned, and that he denies the truth of what has just been said. To apologise to him for the statement or to resist him with argument is equally fatal, for the whole ease and good-temper required for pleasant talk has vanished for that occasion.

§ 57. For this reason, unless the talk consists of confidences between two people who thoroughly understand one another, in which case I hold personal topics to be far the easiest and the most agreeable, it should be our duty to raise if possible the gossip about individuals into reflections upon classes or even principles. Thus if a young lady tells you that such a man is conceited, you may raise the question how far conceit is excusable, or whether it may not be commendable, whether it means a false estimate of poor endowments or a just estimate of considerable attainments, and so forth. Or else you may inquire whether men or women are the more conceited as a rule, and whether Aristotle was not right in setting down over-bashfulness as a vice. Beginning then with the characters of individuals, which is the easiest prologue, and in which somebody will always be ready to start, disengage the general or common feature, and you will not only avoid personalities, but enable those who have no knowledge and interest about the person described to join in the broader discussion of social ethics. And let it not be imagined that because these things have been discussed millions of times they are therefore trite and dull. Just as each succeeding philosopher insists on thinking out again for himself what seems to have been thoroughly exhausted by his predecessors, so every member of society thinks himself capable of deciding over again upon questions which have been settled by thousands of other people to their own satisfaction.

I said just now that when two people only are conversing, personal topics are most suitable, and of all these the confessions of either to the other are the best.

In the first place nothing is so agreeable to most men as to have their own history the object of sympathy, and that is the meaning of the trite adage: Talk to people about themselves, and not about yourself. And again, nothing can be more fascinating than genuine autobiography—I mean confessions of human experience not set down for the public, not trussed and cooked for their use, but the real outspeaking of a human heart. This it is which makes autobiographies so popular as books, though as soon as any one begins to confess to the public, all the real depth and intimacy of his experience vanishes, generally to make way for exhibitions of morbid vanity. It is only one man in a million who has the modesty and the shamelessness, the innocence and the impudence to unveil all his real life to the world of strangers.[1]

[1] I may cite the autobiographies of Benvenuto Cellini and of Alfieri in their complete Italian form as the most real, if not the only real, specimens I know.

Topics of Conversation—Modes of Treatment

§ 58. Finally, we may distinguish the mode in which all subjects may be treated, just as the old rhetoricians divided the various modes of oratory; for, as we said at the outset, conversation may be in theory regarded as informal rhetoric. The old division, then, of orations was based on the form which the company of hearers and speakers assumed. Was it a deliberative assembly, which sat in conclave, as it were, to find out the truth or the right thing to do upon an open question? Then the proper form of eloquence was the *Deliberative,* that of the Senate-house or Parliament suggesting arguments with gravity and modesty,[1] receiving with deference and

[1] I need hardly say that the present Houses of Parliament in England and elsewhere, if we except the House of Lords, will not serve as specimens.

attention the views of others, stimulating all to give their opinions. Was it a judicial court, where the question was a dispute, and the speakers had their line determined as plaintiffs or defendants? Then the form was the *Controversial*, in which each side was bound to make the best of its own case, and the worst of the adversary's; in which each speaker was to bid for the favour of the court, and only limit the violence of his invective by the fear of alienating the judges of the case, and so defeating the object he had in view. Lastly, was the meeting one which merely came together to be impressed or amused by the display of a single speaker, to whom the topic was prescribed, and whose duty it was to excite the emotions and enlist the sympathy of his hearers? Then the proper form was the *Florid*, or *Epideictic*, as they called it, where display was the object, where pomp and ornament were in their proper place.

§ 59. These distinctions are with reasonable reservations clearly applicable to conversation. The best kind is when the subject is discussed by the company as if at an informal council, in which each member gives his opinion, and contributes something to the common stock; where each is not only listened to in turn, but is expected to speak, and where the variety of views and of the expression of them constitutes the very charm of the company. The more people succeed in adopting this form of discussion, the more successful their society will be. The most perfect host and hostess are those who induce all their guests to talk, and elicit even from the silent and the bashful some stray flash of intelligence, which gives additional flavour to the spiritual repast.

It may happen, however, that the topic is taken up by two leading minds in the company, and discussed as a controversy, each putting forth his strength to wrestle with his friendly adversary. Then it may be desirable for the rest to take sides in sympathy, and encourage the conflict of wit or argument. This sort of society may be exceedingly pleasant, provided the disputants keep their temper, and provided they do not monopolise too great a share of the time and attention of the rest. There is hardly a company which will not tire of the discussion of a single subject, however important or interesting. Nevertheless the controversial form is distinctly an agreeable and often highly instructive form of conversation, and many a society of ordinary people attain to the enjoyment of an excellent evening by encouraging two leading spirits to show their powers.

The same good result may be obtained when the company comes together for the purpose of hearing some remarkable person, who is held out as the attraction of the party. It is not conversation, in any real sense, unless it stimulates others to speak; but still we must include in our survey those cases where the funny man, or the Arctic traveller, or the superannuated detective, or the escaped nihilist, undertakes to tell his experiences, and delight us with 'real fiction.' This is truly the epideictic or *show-off* style, in which the solitary speaker is supposed to delight and display himself without a rival, or with a rival silenced before him. Indeed, it is matter of common remark that two or three such talkers are apt to neutralise one another and produce no effect. Each is supposed to be afraid of the other, or jealous of the other, and so wanting in that spontaneity or *abandon* only attained in a congenial atmosphere. This is not my experience of Irish wits, of whom a wise English friend often remarked to me: There is no use in asking one Irishman to dinner; you must ask another to draw him out.

Epilogue

§ 60. The theory of conversation here attempted seems to be completely contained in the foregoing paragraphs, so far as the author has been able to investigate it. No doubt many of his readers will wonder that a subject so interesting can be made so dry, and will complain (in spite of § 5) that he has not given at least a few specimens of what he approves. If he is unable to compose them, why not cull them from the best novel literature of the day? It is, of course, quite easy to give such examples, which can be found in thousands from the comedies of Sheridan to the stories of Lever—who was himself, like Sheridan, a great master of conversation. But who ever profited directly in his own conversation by reading conversations? Who could ever transfer to ordinary intercourse the imaginary dialogues of romance? They may be elaborate and studied, like those of Walter Scott's heroines, and indeed the lovers' dialogues of almost all novelists; or they may be perfectly natural and easy, like those of Charles Lever just referred to. But in either case they are stereotyped in their book, and are useless even as models. One may quote from them an occasional brilliant or foolish remark, as one may from any book, but that is all.

There is always this difficulty about any practice, which has never been reduced to rule, that the laws of it, when set forth in order, seem trivial and dull; nor will the student believe that such valuable and complicated results can be derived from mere truisms. We are quite accustomed to that surprise in the case of logic. The whole system of human reasoning in all its wonderful intricacy is built up from a few general principles in themselves perfectly and necessarily obvious, just as the prose of Ruskin and the poetry of Browning are expressed in combinations of twenty-six letters. But as in this case the theory of composing words is easy enough, and yet the art a mystery, which only very few can ever attain in perfection,—each, too, after his own fashion, and stamped with his own genius,—so the theory of conversation may be reduced to a small number of general observations, and yet the perfect practice of it is a mystery, which defies analysis—one of the myriad manifestations of human genius which all can admire but no one can ever explain.

THE END